Ethnic Relations
Among the People of North-East India

Ethnic Relations Among the People of North-East India

Editor
Prof. N. Joykumar Singh

Centre for Manipur Studies
Manipur University
And
AKANSHA PUBLISHING HOUSE
NEW DELHI-110002

AKANSHA PUBLISHING HOUSE
4649-B/21, Ansari Road
Darya Ganj, New Delhi - 110 002
Email: ektabooks@yahoo.com
Ph.: 23263193/9811582579
Fax: 011-23263193

Ethnic Relations Among the People of North-East India

First Published 2006
ISBN 81-8370-081-0
Reprint 2018

[The responsibility for the facts stated, conclusions reached etc., is entirely that of the Authors. The publisher is not responsible for them, whatsoever.]

PRINTED IN INDIA

Published by M.P. Misra for Akansha Publishing House, New Delhi and Printed at Aryan Enterprises, Delhi

CONTENTS

Preface

Situated between two cultural realms, that of India in the West and the Southeast Asian countries in the east, the Northeast has been experiencing contested identity formations and dynamic ethnic relations for centuries. Ethnic relations in the region is thus associated with its social, cultural, economical, political and historical experiences. They have their ramifications in identity formations, ethnic conflicts and territorial assertions. These ramifications are promoted or even contested on the basis of "unique" histories, cultures and affinities of the people in the region. Such bases are not always free from prejudice and political motivations. This results in contested views on identities of the ethnic groups, their territorial assertions and the conflict situations.

It was in this context that the need to address the different aspects of the ethnic relations in the region was felt. And the Centre for Manipur Studies, Manipur University thus envisaged a seminar on the theme, "Ethnic Relations among the People of the Northeast India with Special Reference to Manipur" to generate a wide spectrum of views on the issue from different cross-sections of the intelligentsia including historians, political scientists, economists, geographers, sociologists, social workers and others. The seminar was held on 10th to 11th November, 2004 at Manipur University. The present volume is a product of the collection of the proceeding papers.

Prof. Gangmumei Kamei's key not address highlights the issue in the context of the geographical, historical and cultural situations of the region. He introduces the historical, economic and religious aspects of ethnic relations, and ethnic tension in Manipur. Prof. Amar Yumnam's paper, "Ethnic Relationship in Manipur: Good, Bad, Good" gives a critical analysis of the economic basis of ethnic relationship in Manipur in different historical epochs. He also examines the implications of such ethnic relations. Konjengbam Meghachandra Singh, in his paper "Ethnic Relations in Manipur: An Urban Experience" explores the relations of the ethnic groups who developed their territorial spaces within the capital city of Manipur. Aheibam Koireng Singh's paper "Dynamics of Kuki-Naga Inter-Group Relations in Manipur: 1992-2000" addresses the genesis, ramifications of the Kuki-Naga conflict in Manipur. Dr. M. Ranjana, in his paper "Socio-Political Relation between the Moirangs and the Ningthoujas during Historical Period" explains the relationship between the two principalities in terms of the social values and practices from the earliest historical times. Dr. M.C. Arun's paper "Ethnicity and Ethnic Fragmentation: The Question of Bishnupriya" gives a critical examination of the process of ethnic amalgamation by which Bishnupriyas became a part of the Manipur society and the fragmentation of the society, that resulted in the 'Bishnupriya-Meitei conflict'. Dr. S. Mangi's paper "The Kuki-Paite Clash (1997-98) in Manipur: A study" is a critical evaluation of the genesis and extent of the Kuki-Paite clash and the various reconciliation processes to resolve it. Dr. Suresh, in his paper "A Comparative Study on Ahom Tai and Meitei Dead Rituals", explores the death rituals of the Tai and Meiteis and the affinities in cultural practices of the two people. Dr. Amal Sanasam's paper "Social Integration in Early Manipur : Some Aspects" analysis the historical circumstances of social integration in ancient Manipur and process of integration among the different communities and clans in both the Hills and the Valleys.

The Centre for Manipur Studies is greatly indebted to Prof. N. Bijoy Singh, Former Vice-Chancellor, Manipur University for his kind and generous initiative in organizing the seminar. The Centre also extends its gratitude to Prof. C. Amuba Singh. Vice-Chancellor of the Manipur University for his generous initiatives in the publication of the proceeding papers. The seminar was made successful by the valuable papers of the contributors. Many research scholars, faculty members and staff of the Centre and the University made painful contributions in the organization of the seminar. The Centre extends its thanks and gratitude to the contributors and all those persons who have contributed in the organization of the seminar. Last, but not the least, the Centre to expresses its indebtedness to Shri M.P. Misra Akansha Publishing House, New Delhi for taking all the initiatives in the publication of the present volume.

PROF. N. JOYKUMAR SINGH
Director
Centre for Manipur Studies
Manipur University

List of Contributors

Arun, M.C. is an Associate Professor in the Department of Anthropology, Manipur University, Manipur. He is a distinguished academician, columnist and playwright. He has contributed in a wide range of fields such as identity issues, women's studies, health, HIV-AIDS, documentaries on social issues, regional history etc. Besides his contributions in professional journals, he has also been engaged by many national bodies such as the ICSSR and the ICMR.

Devi, M Ranjana is a Lecturer in Standard Collage, Imphal. Her area of specialization is ancient history of India. She has contributed in a number of research journals and presented a number of seminar papers on various aspects of the ancient history of Manipur.

Kamei, Gangmumei is former professor of the Department of History, Manipur University, Manipur. He is a distinguished academician and historian of the Northeast. He has authored a number of books on historiography, regional history and identity questions, besides his numerous articles in professional journals. He is also a great social worker.

Sanasam, Amal is a Research Associate in the Centre for Manipur Studies, Manipur University, Manipur. As a sociologist, he is specialized in traditional values, practices and statecraft. He is credited with a number of publications in these aspects. His numerous articles reflect the traditional practices, social problems of the scheduled castes and remote village. He is also specialized in the field of photo-journalism and stays as a free-lancer.

Singh, Konjengbam Meghachandra is a research scholar of the Department of History, Manipur, University, Manipur. He has a geographical background and his area of specialization is urban and regional studies. He has been associated in projects sponsored by national bodies such as the Planning Commission of India and the National Commission for Women.

Singh, Aheibam Koireng is a research scholar of the Department of Political Science, Manipur, University Manipur. His area of specialization is identity questions and conflict resolution. He has been associated in a project on Kuki-Naga conflict and the internally displaced people in Manipur, sponsored by the Indian Council of Social Science Research, New Delhi.

Singh, S. Mangi is an Associate Professor in the Department of Political Science, Manipur University. He is specialized in socio-political problems. Besides his contribution in a number of professional journals, and seminar proceedings, he has also been engaged in a number of projects sponsored by national bodies such as ICSSR and CSDS, New Delhi.

Suresh, L. is a medical practitioner by profession. He has a special knowledge of Tai-Studies with his expertise in the language, culture and environment of the Tais. Being a social worker, he has also contributed in the study of cultural affinities and identity questions.

Yumnam, Amar is a professor of Economic, Manipur University. He is distinguished economist of the region. Besides his contributions in professional journals and other publications he has also been actively engaged in planning and policy-making at the international and national levels. He has been associated with international bodies such as World Bank, UNDP, Asian Development Bank, etc. in various projects.

Ethnic Relation among the People of the North-East with Special Reference to Manipur

— Gangmumei Kamei

A Unique and Strategic Situation

The Northeast is a unique and strategic geographic situation, which is the meeting place of different races and ethnic groups surrounded by China, Bhutan, Bangladesh and Myanmar. India meets Southeast Asia and Central Asia in Northeast India. This is reflected in her ethnic and cultural pluralism.

Ethnic Diversity

The Northeast presents an ethnic diversity which is a part of India's plural society. Diversity is a special feature of the ethnic composition of the racial movements into and across the eastern Himalayas, the Brahmaputra valley and the surrounding great mountain mass during different periods of history from the ancient times to the modern times. The main segments of the population are the Tibeto–Burmans who are also known as the Indo–Mongoloids; the Australoid and Indo–Aryan. The ethnic groups migrated from the southwest China, crossing Tibet, the eastern Himalayas and northern Myanmar. The Indo–Aryans came from the great plains of mainland India.

Ethnic relation among the people is essentially between these three racial groups. But within their broad relation, there are various sub-groups who form the distinct ethnic entities on the basis of language, ethnicity, religion and culture. The greatest ethnic groups are the Bodo–kacharis with about a dozen tribes such as the Garos, Tripuris, Dimasa, Rabha, Mech, Bodo–proper etc. Then came the ancient Austroloids, the Khasi and Jaintias, also the Meities, Nagas, Karbis, Kukis–chins, Mizos, the Ahom, the Indo–Aryan speaking Assamese and various Indian migrant communities like the Bengali, Bihari, Marawari, the Santals and other tea garden tribes who came to northeast India during the British colonial period onwards.

Emergence of the Ethnic State

The ancient states were Pragjyotish and Kamarupa which were established by the Bodo people but later on controlled by the Aryan colonizers from the northern India imposing their rule over the Bodo-speaking tribes. The ancient Meiteis established their Kingdom of Kangleipak(renamed Manipur in the 18th century). The Kacharis established their Kingdom in upper Assam with Dimapur as the capital from the 10th to the 16th century. The Bodo state of Tripura was established in the early middle ages. After decline of the Hindu kingdom of Kamarupa, the Mau-Shans known as Tai-Ahoms migrated to upper Assam from upper Burma and established their kingdom in AD1228. They ruled in Assam from the 13th to the early 19th century. In the 13th century, the Muslims invaded Assam from the west, starting from Bhakhtiyar Khalji's inroads to the large scale Mughal invasion and maintained the sovereignty of Assam under them. In the modern times, with the rise of the Burmese imperialism and the British colonial policy of opening up of the north eastern frontier led to the Anglo–Burmese war (1824-26) which resulted in the conquest of Assam and other principalities. In the 19th century the British conquered all the states and ethnic groups. All the former states were reduced to the states of districts and the tribes were constituted into administrative units, districts and sub-divisions. Only Manipur, Tripura and the Khasi States could maintain their distirct political entities under the British paramountcy. In the post indepencence periods, Assam was balkanized into four states Assam, Nagaland, Meghalaya and Mizoram. Manipur and Tripura were upgraded to statehood; so also Arunachal Pradesh

Manipur: A Land of Homogenity and Heterogenity.

Manipur stands out as a unique state in the whole region. Manipur is a multi ethnic state. Her population consists of the Meiteis, the Nagas, the Kuki-Chins, and the Muslim. These are also migrant communities from mainland India like the Bengalis, Biharis, Sikhs, Marwaris, Nepali, recently the Tamils. Manipur is a meeting place of different racial groups. The movements of people into the State from the prehistorcal times down to the present is a great historical phenomenon. The hill state with a beautiful oval valley in the middle attracted various people for trade, wealth and glory. Manipur was never an isolated country. She is the gateway between India and south East Asia.

Underneath the outward ethnic diversity, these are elements of affinity. The indigenous Meiteis, the Nagas and Kuki Chin are all Tibeto Burman racially and linguistically. They speak different linguistic sub-group of the Tibeto Burman family. Linguists and Anthropologist have found and established the root of the Tibeto Burman family. However, the Meitei(Manipuri) has a highly developed literature and is recognized as the Modern Language in Indian universities and a regional language included in the Eigth Schedule of the Indian Constitution. There are affinities in the roots of the Meitei, Naga and Kuki-Chin languages. Because of the common origin of Tibeto Burman family who migrated from Southwest China Upper Myanmar of the state, there is also ethnic affinity among these communities of

Manipur. In the course of their long history there grew up close cultural relationship among the ethnic groups of Manipur particularly between the Meitei and Nagas; and later on the Kukis. The folklore prevalent in the hills and valley relates the close contact between the Naga tribes and the Meiteis and also with the kings. The ethnic and cultural relation between the Meitei clans and the Tangkhuls are well known. The relation between the Moirang principality with the Rongmei Moyon-Monsang and Anals are all recorded facts. The intermarriage between the Meitei culture heroes who were deified into gods-preserved in the tradition of marriage between Soraren of Koubru and a girl of Harok Konthou tribe (now identified as Konthoujam Lairema), Wangbren, a Meitei God of Sugnu with an Anal girl of Anal Khullen is indicative of the strong link. The Tangkhul-Meitei tradition of origin from Khangkhui cave and the migration of the younger brother Meitei in the valley is a popular tradition. The tradition of Kabui Salang Maiba(Ram ngampou) of Ningthi village in the Khamba-Thoibi epic is supported by History. The marriage of Meitei kings with Naga girls (for example Maram Naga) is history. The Nongpok-Ningthou-Panthoibi tradition in the LaiHaraoba festival (Tangkhul Saba) is the living proof of the ancient connection between the Meitei and Tangkhuls.

Over and above the close ethnic and cultural links the various ethnic groups are bound by economic interdependence. There were barter trades in the traditional economy. And this barter trade produced a close social linkage. In the nineteenth century, there were a large number of tribal converted into Hinduism and absorbed into Meitei social fold. In the post–independence period with the development modern education and relation facilitated by of government service and trade, there are now a lot of intermarriages between the Meiteis and tribes. Most of the major families of the Meitei have tribal daughter-in-laws.

Economic Relation

North East India and Manipur are on the international trade route. In ancient times there were brisk trade between North East India and China on the one hand and the Roman world on the other. The Roman and Greek writers, especially Claudius Ptolemy in his *Geographika* and Periplus of the Erytherian sea by an unnamed author refer to the tribal communities in eastern India like Kirhadia(Kiratas), Nangalogae(Nagas), Besatau etc. And the brisk trade with the Roman Empire in the second century AD through South India has been referred to. The excavations at Ambari in modern Guwahati confirm the Roman trade. The region also served as trade route between China and Central Asia. Within the region, there were trade between hill men of the eastern Himalayas with the people living in the north bank of the Brahmaputra. The Garos, Khasis and Jaintias were great traders with the Bengali traders in the Surma valley. The Nagas, particularly the Angamis, the Lhotas and the Aos are great trading tribes. There were regular trade flow between the Brahmaputra valley and upper Burma across the Patkai mountain; that preceded the Ahom migration and conquest of Assam. Manipur was on the trade route between India and Burma. The international caravan trade between Manipur and Burma continued throughout history with their hostile relations. The Mizos are great traders who have connections with the Bengalis of the Bengal-plains, the Chins hills of Burma, Assam and Manipur.

Since the colonial period with development of road and communication, especially railways, the economic relations among the people of Northeast have greatly increased .

Religious Aspect of the Ethnic Relation

The indigenous people of the region have their own religious belief and practices. But the religious groups in mainland India have brought Vedic Hinduism, and Buddhism to region. But from within the region was developed Tantrik

Hinduism with the Temple of Kamakhya as the centre. Then Vajrayana or Tantrik Budhism grew up. In the medieval times, Islam was brought by the Muslim invaders who came along with Muslim immigrants to Assam. After the British conquest in the nineteenth century, Chritianity was introduced and the hill people had accepted this foreign faith. While Hinduism and Islam were confined to the Brahmaputra and Manipur valley, Buddhism was brought in from Tibet and upper Myanmar.

In the medieval period there was a strong Vaisnavite reform movement, popularly known as Bhakti movement under the leadership of Shri Shankardeva. Under his inspiring leadership Vaisnavism was spread to many tribal communities of Assam like , Bodo, Kachari, Chutya, Baraha etc. Even many Nagas accepted vaisnavism. Some tribes of Arunachal Pradesh still follow Vaisnavism. Shakta Hinduism was accepted by the Ahom rulers and there was conflict between the Shakta Hindus and the Vaisnavites. Manipur valley, Tripura and Cachar accepted Vaisnavism. Amidst these well-established religion, there are the indigenous religious traditions flourishing. Mention may be made of the Sanamahi religious cult of the Meiteis who are found in Manipur and Assam; the Seng Khasi of Meghalaya, the Donyi Polo of Arunachal and the Ting Kao Ragwang Chapriak among the Zeliangrong people of Manipur Assam and Nagaland and the Brahma Dharma among the Bodos of Assam. Except the belligerent Christian proselytism, there was a harmonious religious relation among the people of the region.

Ethnic Tension

However during the post independence period, there was tension between various ethnic groups in the region. The first occasion was the official language issue. Assamese as the official language and Bengalis as the District level official language of Barak valley. There are conflicts between the

Bengalis and Tripuris in Tripura, the Kuki-Naga conflict in Manipur is quite well known. There was anti Santal riot in the Bodo-land, the conflict between the Kukis , Hmars and Dimasa in North cachar hills. These ethnic conflicts have posed a great danger to the ethnic relationship in the region. The basic cause of these conflicts is the question of possession of lands. While the earlier indigenous settlers are jealously guarding their rights to land, the new comers have to struggle for livelihood. While the Kuki-Naga conflict has been resolved, the Tripuri-Bengali tension remains. The Dimasa are still struggling for the protection of their homeland; the clash of interest between the Garo and the Khasi reflects the simmering ethnic situation in the region.

2

Ethnic Relationships in Manipur: Good, Bad, Good

— **Amar Yumnam**

Introduction

The issue of inter-ethnic relationships now inhabit almost every academic discourse in the social sciences in Manipur. This is to be welcomed given the fact that, despite being small in geographical space, the State is characterised by plurality of ethnic groups. But, unfortunately for all of us, the discourse has arisen in the context of heightened inter-ethnic tensions in the State. Nevertheless, the fact that it has taken the form of an involved dialogue provides the silver lining to the emerging scenario. I shall attempt in this paper to articulate the economic reasons for the present not so calm relationships among the various ethnic groups in the State. Before I proceed I should explain my understanding of a good or bad relationship. My understanding of this is necessarily contextual. I would call an ethnic relationship a good one if all the diverse groups function as usual, and do not articulate and express any reservations, either orally or physically, on the dealings with the other group. Not only would the various groups express the relationships as good, but also seem to be good. Any untoward incident involving persons of two different ethnic groups would not lead to any inert-ethnic misunderstanding, and there would be endogenous processes in place with which each community would address such issues without involving the other group; even if an individual starts articulating issues against the other community in terms of ethnicity, it would never reach the organisational level. On the other hand, an inter-ethnic relationship would be a bad one if each group develops suspicion of the other, and articulates and expresses, either orally or physically, reservations against the other group for any social, political or economic outcome. Any untoward incident involving persons of two different ethnic groups would have a tendency to turn into an inter-ethnic tension, and the endogenous forces for addressing such issues within a group would be weak.[1] In such an atmosphere even if an individual does not articulate and try to convert an incident into an inter-ethnic one, there would bo ready organisations for doing so.

The conventional understanding of modernisation and development is that ethnicity would disappear gradually and classes would emerge instead. There would be no sharpening of ethnic identity and ethnic based articulations. Recent social capital literature establishes that maintaining an individualised specific identity would be a very costly affair.[2] Ethnicity can serve, in appropriate circumstances, as a social capital for promoting modernisation. Ethnicity can, on the other hand, be even mobilised for political ends, violence included.

The Good Past

That the ethnic relationships were good in the past is not disputed by any party. In fact, the most dominant nostalgias are the sharing of ancestral origins and the direct person to person interaction till the recent past. Though many imperfections of these historical relationships, particularly the one between the valley-dwelling larger numbered Meeteis and the various ethnic groups settling mostly in the hills, have been pointed out recently, yet the commonality of ancestral origins and mutual festivities in the historical past are not questioned. The royal chronicles and the oral history traditions are full of anecdotes and stories of such mutuality of existence, survival, cooperation, and commonality of ancestral origins.[3]

The Bad Present

My concern in this paper, however, is not with the *good past,* but with the *bad present*. I shall attempt, as mentioned earlier, to give an economic explanation why the *bad present* has emerged out of the *good past*. There are two aspects in this. First, the *good past* had, on hindsight, elements of its own backlash. Secondly, the various interactions in the recent present have not served the purpose of an integrated development of a multi-ethnic economy. There is no tight demarcation in the time line of these two aspects. In fact, elements for the backlash had continued till recent past as well.

The backlash: The backlash causes are fundamentally sociological if we look at it historically and even the articulations are fundamentally sociological. Historically, the Meeties have inhabited the location-friendly valley area and have been the ruling as well as the more advanced of the different ethnic groups in the State. On hindsight, the attitude and treatment of the other ethnic groups inhabiting the hills by the Meeties had not been one of equality and inclusion. This naturally had created a certain kind of alienation and feeling for vengeance. This atmosphere would not have lasted if we could evolve an interactive economy whereby a common future and a common growth were built-in. But unfortunately this had not happened. This takes us to the second aspect of the *bad present*. I shall now turn to this.

Multi-ethnic economy: The foundations of the traditional strength of the Meeteis are:

a. The economically more friendly spatial structure of the valley where they inhabit;

b. The more rather than less homogeneity of their population as compared to the widely heterogeneous ethnic groups in the hills; and

c. The second feature of homogeneity was reinforced by the factor of larger population, whose sustenance was made easy by the fertile valley soil.

The manifestation of these features in the general conduct of the Meetei populace (particularly of the Meetei Brahmins and the staunch Vaishnavaites after the adoption of Hinduism), coupled with the non-inclusive nature of development in the historical past, must have imbibed to the smaller ethnic groups in the hills a desire for homogeneity and population multiplication in order to extract a larger share of the pie as well as assert a sense of pride and dignity. What is unfortunate for all is that these tendencies have too long been allowed to continue along ethnically divisive lines with accentuated political, ethnical and sociological articulations. Even after full five and a half decades of planning efforts, there has been no attempt to give an economic turn and an economic articulation of these issues. These have hampered the emergence of an economic momentum for growth which could take all upward. This is what I turn to now.

The economy of Manipur can be viewed as a loose conglomerate of very small, both in terms of population and economic, open economies. The macro–economy of Manipur is such that it cannot fully co-opt and incorporate the numerous small economies prevailing at pockets of ethnicity and space. In other words, Manipur's macroeconomy consists of various local economies in the sense that, despite the potential and real free mobility of labour and other factors, the level of interaction is such that the overall interdependence within the region/sub-region spaces and population do not decide the overall economic fate of the internally homogeneous and externally heterogeneous population groups and spaces.

It is in such an atmosphere that Manipur has experienced growth slowdown, if not collapse, right from the 1970s to till today, despite the short growth spurt in the early 1970s. This period also corresponds to the period during which the credibility of the state as an institution has suffered a sharp decline.[4] Due to the enforcement of rule of state law rather than rule of law, each ethnic group was force-mobilised to be always on alert to protect itself and reduce the damages from the brutalities of the enforcement of rule of state law. Now we had before us the following realities:

a. The sociological reality of non-inclusive society;

b. The economic reality of non-inclusive growth and growth slowdown; and

c. The political reality of lack of credibility of the state.

As a result of the interplay of the above factors the various groups did not visualise any economic benefit from identifying with and working for the larger macro–economy of Manipur. Now these are necessary and sufficient conditions for the ethnic-based articulations and mobilisations to surface as well as gain momentum in a multi-ethnic society like Manipur's. The primordial identity now becomes the only identity for rallying around for political and economic reasons as well.[5] In other words, the primordial identity has become the instrumental variable for all articulations – political, sociological and economic. Unfortunately for Manipur, the use of this identity has been made even more convenient and forceful by the districting process in the State. The districting of the State has made it possible for the primordial identities to develop a concept of homeland as distinct from Manipur as well. The unfortunate fall-out of these processes is the fast decline in democratic values, norms and practices by mugging debate and dissent within and dialogue with outside.[6]

The Good Future

Having attempted to explain how I view the recent developments as bad and why these have become bad, it is now incumbent on my part how the good future is being visualised by me. *If it is pitch dark in the night, the morning cannot be far away.* There are various reasons for my visualising a good future. First, the dominant majority group now seems to have realised, if not openly admit, her historical follies. So there are now many moves both by individuals and organisations to undo the historical damage through positive action. Secondly, there seems now emerging a certain kind of backlash to the decline of democratic norms within ethnic groups, and slowly but surely a certain culture of tolerance for positive criticism is evolving. Thirdly, the till-now-silent minority of those vouching for good ethnic relationships is now subtly making its voice heard. Fourthly, the macroeconomy of Manipur has of late started acquiring a character of endogenous performance. Well just as there were elements for the bad phase to come, these are conditions for the good relationship to emerge and prevail. Prevail definitely it will be for we have learnt at our own cost that nobody gains from a bad inter-ethnic relationship. Diversity is good for economic performance, witness Mumbai and New York.

NOTES

1. I would not say non-existent because, at any point of time and in any social context, there would always be persons who would unequivocally articulate, vouch and work for good inter-ethnic relationships.
2. For a discussion on the economics of identity, see Bodenhorn, Howard and Christopher S. Ruebeck, (2003), *The Economics of Identity and the Endogeneity of Race NBER. Working Paper 1962.*

3. References on this are galore. Kindly see *Cheitharol Kumpaba* and the various works on *Lai Haraoba*. The other papers on this volume also contain many references on this aspect.
4. On the relationship between state credibility and development, see Borner, Silvio, Aymo Brunetti and Beatrice Weder, (1995), *Political Credibility and Economic Development,* St. Martin's Press.
5. In this context, it would be rewarding to read, Green, Elliott D., (2005), What is an Ethnic Group? Political Economy, Constructivism and the Common Language Approach to Ethnicity, *Development Studies Institute Working Paper Series No. 05-57,* London School of Economics.
6. For a general discussion on such issues, see Hirschman, A.O., (1970), *Exit, Voice and Loyalty: Responses to Decline in Firms, Organizations and States,* Harvard University Press, Mass.

3

Ethnic Relations in Manipur: An Urban Experience

— Konjengbam M. Singh

Introduction

The study of ethnic relations in an urban area needs special attention as urbanisation and ethnicity are both complimentary and contradictory. The two are complimentary in the sense that urban areas, specially the capital cities or towns, offer avenues for the establishment of ethnic or community neighbourhoods, enabling different ethnic groups or communities to coexist, thus forming ethnic mosaics. Urbanisation and ethnicity are also contradictory as attributes of ethnicity such as shared space, close kinship links, shared religions and moral values, social cohesion, mutual trust and cooperation etc. are being replaced in an urban area by such attributes of urbanism as anonymity, individualism and competition. Segregation of ethnic or racial groups or communities, interaction between these groups, dominance and even succession of certain groups are facets of ethnic relations in urban centres. In this paper I propose to make an attempt to explore the theoretical postulations on the arrangement of ethnic groups in urban centres and the formation and transformation of ethnic or community neighbourhoods in Imphal, the capital city of Manipur, in the historical perspective.

Urbanization: A Theoretical Perspective

Urbanization is a very complex and multifaceted phenomenon. The process of urbanization has temporal, spatial and functional dimensions. It also has many facets expressed in all the three dimensions. McGee[1] identified three main facets of urbanization namely, demographic, economic and social. Urbanization as a demographic process refers to an increase in the percentage of urban population in the total population. Bose[2] defined urbanization as 'an increase in the proportion of the urban population (U) to the total population (T) over a period of time'. Such an increase in the proportion of urban population may result from an increase in the number of urban areas or an increase in the size of urban areas or both.

The economic aspect of urbanization refers to the shift of an economy from rural to non-rural. Mandal and Peters[3] argued that 'the process of urbanization includes the change of economy which may be from forest to agriculture, agriculture to manufacturing-oriented production centres and centres of exchange of goods'. Urbanization involves improvement in infrastructure, emergence of new industries, diversification of occupation and thus the provision of new economic opportunities.

The social aspect of urbanization includes new social orders produced by urbanization. The bonds of kinship, of neighbourliness, and the sentiments arising out of living together for generations under a common folk tradition are likely to be absent, or at best, relatively weak in an aggregate, the member of which have diverse origins and backgrounds (carter 1972).[4] Concentration of people of diverse origins leads to differentiation and the individual earns a new status determined by his ability and effort rather than by his birth.

Individual relations become more impersonal and superficial, competition and formal control mechanisms substitute the bonds of solidarity.

Urbanization, thus involves not only population concentration which is a way of ordering a population to attain a certain level of subsistence and security in a given environment, but it also includes the economic and social changes associated with it.

Ethnic Groups within Cities

Ethnicity and ethnic groups are among the most difficult terms to define in social sciences. The etymology of the term ethnicity dates back to ancient Greece where 'ethnos' referred to 'people' or 'nation'. In contemporary usage, ethnicity is seen as both a way in which individuals define their personal identity and a type of social stratification that emerges when people form groups based on their real or perceived origins[5]. The problem in defining the terms 'ethnicity' and 'ethnic group' is that different groups based their identity on different traits. As Jordan and Rowntree[6] observed, for some such as Amish, it is religion, for the Swiss–American it is ancestral nationality; for the blacks it is race; for the German–American it is ancestral language; for the French–Canadian it is mother tongue; for the Cuban–American it is political philosophy; for the Appalachian southerner it is folk culture. The main unifying factor differs from one group to another.

Ethnic groups are the keepers of distinctive cultural traditions and they are also the focal point of various kinds of interaction. They offer social security and cultural reinforcement among the members, so essential for minorities. Ethnic groups tend to live in more or less exclusive localities called neighbourhoods. The establishment of such ethnic neighbourhoods is prevalent throughout human history. 'America's Little Switzerland' in Wisconsin was founded by Swiss immigrants in 1845. Bohemian immigrants started their settlement in Wilber (the Czech Capital of Nebraska) in 1865. 'Black Belts', 'China Towns', and many other such ethnic neighbourhoods prevail in contemporary urban centres including metropolitan cities. While these ethnic neighbourhoods offer cultural security and reinforcement, so essential for minorities, they can also give rise to suspicion, friction, distrust, clannishness, and even violence.

Neighbourhoods, Ethnic Neighbourhoods and Ghettos

There is not a consensus among the social scientists, planners and policy makers on what neighbourhoods are. Keller[7] gave an ecological perspective while defining neighbourhoods as 'place with physical and symbolic boundaries'. While others defined the term from both social and ecological perspective. Hallman[8], for instance, defined the term as 'a limited territory within a larger urban area, where people inhabit dwellings and interact socially'. Galster[9] attempted a holistic definition that incorporates eight attributes. He defined the term as 'the bundle of spatially based attributes associated with clusters of residences, sometimes in conjunction with other land uses'. The eight attributes he emphasised are: (i) structural characteristics of residential and non-residential buildings, (ii) infrastructural characteristics, (iii) class status characteristics, (iv) tax/public service package characteristics, (v) environmental characteristics, (vi) Proximity characteristics, (vii) social interactive characteristics and (viii) sentimental characteristics. Neighbourhood thus can be look upon as having one or more of the above characteristics.

Kearns and Parkinson[10] identified three scales of neighbourhoods. The smallest area is the home area; which is 5-10 minutes walk from one's home and the psycho-social purposes of neighbourhood is strongest. The next higher level is 'locality' where residential activities, social status and position are important. The highest level is 'urban districts' or 'region' which is landscape of social and economic opportunities. Though neighbourhood in cities are established on the basis of varied attributes, neighbourhoods based on ethnic attributes are the most prominent and distinctive ones. As Jordan and Rowntree[11] observed, 'An ethnic neighbourhood is an area within a city where members of an ethnic group are concentrated'. Such ethnic neighbourhoods are found across the world throughout the history of human civilization. American cities drew heavily on Ireland and eastern and southern Europe for their ethnic neighbourhoods. Catholic Irish, Italians, Poles and East European Jews became the main urban ethnic groups. In the United States, these groups were later joined by French, Canadians, southern blacks, Puerto Ricans, Philiopines, Chinese, Appalachian whites, Amerindians, Cuban and other groups not of European birth. Thus Jordan and Rowntree conceived of these ethnic neighbourhoods as 'a voluntary community where people reside by choice'.[12]

We can make a distinction between 'ethnic neighbourhood' and 'ghetto' though the two terms are used synonymously and interchangeably. 'The term *ghetto* has traditionally been used to describe an area within the city where a certain ethnic group has been forced to live. The term perhaps originated in medieval Venice, where Jews were required to live in an undesirable part of the city near the ironworks'.[13] Later this term has been used to denote an underprivileged neighbourhood, in any urban place.

Urbanization and Ethnic Neighbourhood in Imphal

The generalized ethnic mapping of Manipur is that Manipur has three major ethnic groups viz., the *Meities* of the valley and the *Nagas* and *Kukis* of the surrounding hills. This generalized ethnic mapping finds its ground and validity in two aspects of distribution of ethnic groups. First, each of the three major ethnic groups has geographical territories where it is numerically dominant. Second, this generalized ethnic mapping is to a great extent shaped by the historical and even proto-historical geographical distribution of the ethnic groups, centuries before the formation of ethnic mosaics and advent of rampant urbanization. Kabui[13] observed, 'Manipur has three major ethnic groups. The Meiteis of the valley, the Nagas and Kukis of the surrounding hill tribes'. This and other similar observations equate 'numerical dominance' to 'ethnic exclusivity'. Thereby equating ethnic groups and territory and ignoring the composite ethnic mosaic particularly in the valley of Manipur and more specifically in the capital city of Imphal. It is in this perspective that the present paper attempts to address the issue of ethnic relations in the capital city of Manipur.

Imphal, since the beginning, has been the centre of 'acculturation' and 'assimilation', though the early history of Imphal was marked more by assimilation than by acculturation. Acculturation, which became more prominent in the latter part of Imphal's history, produced a composite society or a mosaic of ethnic groups. In the early period, Manipur was inhabited by several principalities or tribes, important of them being seven principalities viz. the *Meities, Khaba-Nganba, Chenglei, Angom, Khuman, Luwang* and *Moirang*. Several other tribes merged with one or the other of these seven principalities in course of time. In several centuries that followed, the Meities (or the Ningthoujas) established supremacy over the rest and absorbed them one by one. And 'Meitei became the common nomenclature for all of them'.[14]

Meities believe that the first settlement was on the top of Koubru mountain, considered as the God's abode. Subsequently, the seven principalities or clans began to settle in different parts of the valley. Each of the seven clans was headed by a chieftain (king of Piba) and used to function like that of the city states of ancient Greek.[15] Manikchand also observed that the seven principalities were closely knit and allied ones, once settled in different parts of Manipur, each independent of each other.[16] Imphal came under the most dominant principality, the Ningthouja, which made its capital at 'Kangla' at Imphal. The ancient capital of Manipur is believed to be at the site of the present 'Kangla' at Imphal. 'Kangla' was a walled area built for the ruling class. The common people lived outside the walled area. Later the settlement area expanded further. When the British arrived in Manipur, the whole of Imphal including the outlying villages was considered as urban. Since 1901 when a regular census was started in Manipur, Imphal, has been considered as a town. Till 1961 Imphal was the only town in Manipur. Thus Imphal is the oldest urban centre in Manipur. To a common man in Manipur, Imphal is synonymous with an urban centre.[17] The urban population of Imphal was 72234 persons in 1901. This was 25.39 percent of the total population of the State. According to the 2001 census the urban population of Imphal is 245967 persons comprising about 12 percent of total population of the state.[18]

The urban population of Imphal comprises of many communities that have different ethnic affiliations. As Kabui observed, 'From the prehistoric times down to the present day, Manipur has always attracted migrants and colonisers from outside.'[19] As the state was a trade route between India and South East Asia, it attracted migrants from both the west (Nongchup Haram or Westerners) and the east (Nongpok Haram or Easterners). Most of the easterners have been absorbed in the Manipuri society. The westerners and much later the tribals from the hills settled down in Imphal in distinctive neighbourhoods. During the pre-colonial period, most of the westerners who settled down in Manipur were mainly religious or trading communities. The Brahmins, the Muslims, the Bengalis, the Biharis and the Marwaris are important among them. Right from the pre-colonial period, many tribal communities also started to settle in Imphal.

Specially during the colonial period they established their own neighbourhoods. Of these the more or less exclusive Kabui neighbourhoods in Imphal such as Majorkhul, Kakhulong, Ragailong etc. may be mentioned. And in recent decades 'tribals from the hills, specially Government employees and contractors had settled down at Imphal'.[20] Important among the recently developed neighbourhoods are Deulahland, Chekon, Haokip Veng etc.

The ethnic neighbourhoods in Imphal are thus structured and conditioned by their history, urbanization and its associated social, economic and demographic processes and even the dynamic ethnic relations in the state. The Rongmei villages of Manipur rendered Lallup service to the king. These Rongmei villages stand out today as the most distinctive and exclusive ethnic neighbourhoods in Imphal city. Traditional institutions and practices still prevail in these neighbourhoods and their exclusivity is not much deteriorated, compared with other neighbourhoods, though many of them are in the heart of the city. Such exclusivity is rather absent in the neighbourhoods of the business communities including Marwaris, Bengalis, Punjabis, etc. and the tribal communities of the of the Kuki-Chin group. The Meiteis, as the biggest community, live mostly in more or less exclusive Leikais or the traditional neighbourhoods but kinship based Leikais, which traditionally formed the basic unit of settlement, are deteriorated. Community-based and even mixed neighbourhoods become prominent.

The important issue to be addressed in this context is the sceptical view towards the mixed neighbourhoods that lack exclusivity. These mixed neighbourhoods in Imphal are often looked upon as ghettos, or 'black spots'. In the United States, the increase in Black population in white neighbourhoods is conceived as a signed of urban deterioration by many white residents. They even anticipate an increase in crime, drug abuse and immoral acts in such situation. Such anticipation is not an exception in Manipur. The mixed neighbourhoods are looked upon as areas where anonymity is accompanied by all forms of vices. Riajuddin Choudhuri, a retired History Lecturer, of Hafiz Hatta, a Manipur Muslim neighbourhood in Imphal city, gave anonymity and the breakdown in traditional institutions as the causes of deterioration in urban living in mixed neighbourhoods. [21] He was of the opinion that ethnic neighbourhoods are more manageable than the mixed one.

Here two cases of provision of ethnic quota in residential allocation in urban areas, as observed by Sin[22] can be examined. With the influx of migrants in the 1960s and 1970s, Britain operated several national-level dispersal policies. Perceiving the growing concentration of Afro-Caribbean's and South Asians in the inner and middle rings of the city as a problem, the city council felt that racial integration would be facilitated by spreading the black population thinly among the white population. This rationale was however found to be based on the hostility of white tenants towards the black tenants. The controversial policy was abandoned in 1975. Singapore's use of ethnic quotas, on the other hand, was aimed at keeping communities 'racially balanced or diverse'. This was done by allotting public housing keeping in view the ethnic proportions in the different regions of the country. Though the policy was expected to be very successful as 86 percent of the population in the country lived in public housing, yet, it was found that the impact was not felt on the group(s) it was intended for. Thus ethnic quota policy in maintaining ethnic neighbourhoods proves to be fatal as certain communities are favoured at the cost of others.

However, attempts to maintain and resurrect ethnic neighbourhoods in two advanced and industrialised countries in as late as 1970s and 1990s by adopting national housing policies explain the significance of ethnic neighbourhoods in urban planning and ethnic relations. In the two cases mentioned above, the intended goals were diverted by the informed knowledge of the interest groups. However, ethnic neighbourhoods are considered across the world as favourable places to live in urban areas. Emotional bonds, mutual trust, cooperation and social collusion give a sense of belonging in a hitherto hostile urban environment. Further the dynamic ethnic relations in the larger context have their bearings on ethnic neighbourhoods in the city. In Manipur, the infamous Kuki-Naga conflict produced a new equilibrium in the ethnic neighbourhoods in Imphal city. At the special Kuki Tribal Leaders' Meet in 1993, the minutes of discussion stated, 'Many Kukis are wandering about in the capital city without any shelter'.[23] These Kukis were driven out of the hill districts dominated by the Nagas. Such conflict produces the sudden growth in the ethnic neighbourhoods. Rehanurddin Choudhuri, The Sub-Divisional Officer of Kakching Sub-Division (Thoubal District), a resident of Hafij Hatta, even cited many newly emerged tribal villages in the city while others expanded rapidly.[24] Keisamthong (Kabui Village) and Minuthong (Kabui Village), for instance recorded only 382 and 190 persons respectively in 1961.[25] However during the last four decades the population of these two neighbourhoods multiplied to a great extent.

Thus, in the context of the rapid population growth in the ethnic neighbourhoods and the associated transformations in them on the one hand, and the dynamic ethnic relations in the state, the study of ethnic neighbourhoods needs a special focus. Equating territory and ethnic groups at a larger scale reduces the scope for such studies. However, the intra-urban ethnic groups, found in the ethnic neighbourhoods, call for special attention. Cities offer the avenues for the co-existence of ethnic groups. At the same time cities dilute the traditional social institutions and practices through acculturation and assimilation. Yet, there is a quest for ethnic neighbourhoods the world over, even in the most advanced countries. These ethnic neighbourhoods need demarcation and regulation, for the traditional social institutions in these ethnic neighbourhoods cannot be replaced at any scale by formal institutions. And deterioration in the ethnic neighbourhoods in terms of ethnic composition may even destabilise the ethnic groups and the composite urban ethnic mosaic.

NOTES

1. Mc.Gee, T.G. 1971. *The Urbanization Process in the Third World: Explorations in Search of a Theory.* London: Bell. p. 15.
2. Bose, Ashish. 1978. *India's Urbanization 1901-2001.* New Delhi: Tata McGraw-Hill Publishing Company Limited. p.3.
3. Mandal, R.B. and G.L. Peters (Eds.). 1981. *Urbanization and Regional Development.* New Delhi: Concept Publishing Company. p. 3.
4. Carter, Harold. 1972. *The Study of Urban Geography.* London: Edward Arnold. p. 26.
5. Johnston, R.J. etal. (Eds.) 2000. The *Dictionary of Human Geography.* Fourth Edition. Oxford: Blackwell Publishers Ltd. p. 235.
6. Jordan, Terry G. and Lester Rowntree. 1979. *The Human Mosaic.* New York: Harper & Row Publishers. p. 295.
7. Keller, S. 1968. *The Urban Neighbourhood.* New York: Random House.
8. Hallman, H.W. 1984. *Neighbourhoods: Their Place in Urban Life.* Beverly Hills, CA: Sage Publications.
9. Galster, George 2001. On the Nature of Neighbourhood. *Urban Studies.* 38(12): 2111-2124.
10. Kearns, Ade and Michael Parkinson. 2001. The Significance of Neighbourhood. Urban Studies. 38(12): 2103-2110.
11. Jordan, Terry G. and Lester Rowntree. *Op.cit.* p. 299.
12. *Ibid.* p. 302.
13. Kabui, Gangmumei. 1988. Glimpses of Land and People of Ancient Manipur. In Naorem Sanajaoba (ed.), *Manipur Past and Present.* Vol. 1. Mittal Publications. p.12.

14. Manikchand, Konsam. 1988. The Evolution of the Meitei State (A Confederacy through the last two Millennia). In: Naorem Sanajaoba (ed.), *Manipur Past and Present.* Vol. I. p. 147.
15. Laiba, M.T. 1992. *The Geography of Manipur.* Imphal: Public Book Store. p. 4-5.
16. Manikchand, Konsam. *Op. cit.* p. 147.
17. Singh, L. Tombi. 1995. Urbanization in Manipur: An Analysis in Retrospect. In J.B. Ganguly (ed.), *Urbanization and Development in North-East India: Trends and Policy Implications.* New Delhi: Deep and Deep Publications. p. 208.
18. Census of India. 2001.
19. Kabui, Gangmumei. 1991. Imphal – A Short Historical Account. Apprendix. In: Lal Dena (ed.), *History of Modern Manipur (1826-1949).* New Delhi : Orbit Publishers – Distributors. p. 211.
20. *Ibid.* p. 212.
21. Riajuddin Choudhuri was formerly a lecturer of History at G.P. Women's College and the Post Graduate Centre of Jawaharlal Nehru University at Imphal. He was interviewed on 31st October, 2004.
22. Sin, Chih Hoong, 2002. The Quest for a Balanced Ethnic Mix: Singapore's Ethnic Quota Policy Examined. *Urban Studies.* 39(8): 1347–1374.
23. Anniversary Souvenir of the Kuki Inpi Manipur (KIM). 1994. p. 3.
24. Interviewed on 31st Oct., 2004.
25. Census of India. 1961. Vol. XXII. Manipur. Part VI. *Village Survey Monograph. No. 2 and 7.*

4

Dynamics of Kuki-Naga Inter-Group Relations in Manipur: 1992 – 2000

— Aheibam Koireng Singh

In Manipur, the two major tribal groups by the current nomenclatures are the Kukis and the Nagas. Here in this paper, Naga is used to mean a cluster of tribes namely, Anal, Maring, Moyon, Monsang, Lamkang, Poumai, Tangkhul, Mao, Maram, Thangal, Zeilangrong (Zemei, Liangmei, Rongmei, Puimei), Kharam and Tarao. The major Kuki-chin tribes of Manipur are Thadou, Paite, Gangte, Simte, Vaiphei, Hmar, Zou and Tedim-chin, etc. But not all the tribes of Kuki-chin groups were involved in the conflict. The conflict was succinctly between the Thadou speaking Kukis and the Nagas.

Rivalries were not totally absent in the traditional relationship of the Kukis and the Nagas.The colonial British Government made use of the traditional Naga-Kuki feuds for their strategic and imperial interest.[1] The Kuki-Naga feuds are evident from the fact that the Naga Armed Revolution of 1956 provided them an opportunity to retaliate against the Kukis for their historical grudge.[2] During the period from 1956 to September 1964, the Naga armed volunteers devastated nearly 60 Kuki villages in Tamenglong and

Ukhrul Sub-Divisions.[3] In Nagaland,Kukis did not experienced such organised offences at that time . They were accepted as indigenous peoples of Nagaland. Kuki was also one of the constituent tribes which formed the Naga Club in 1918 and there was one Kuki among the signatories of the Memorandum submitted to the Simon Commission 1929 by the Naga Club. In 1946, two Kuki candidates were elected as members of NNC. Sukhohen Kuki also served as member of the Constitution Drafting Committee of NNC. Moreover, in the Naga Voluntary Plebiscite completed on 16 May,1951 the Kukis voted in favour of Naga independence.[4]

Many reasons were given for the outbreak of the clashes in 1992.Rishang Keishing, the Deputy Chief Minister at that time was of the opinion that land disputes due to encroachment, imposition of heavy taxes in hill areas for the last so many years and demand for Homeland from both sides were responsible for the outbreak of the clashes.[5] R.K. Dorendro, during his tenure as Chief Minister has experienced both the Kuki-Naga clash and the Meitei-Pangal communal frenzy. He was able to contain the later at a very short time.However the former continued to occur with intense magnitude and grave dimension.In an interview appeared in *The Freedom*, he opined that the former was difficult to contain as they had a history of long standing rivalry since the distant past.[6] The then Governor of Manipur, Lt. General V.K. Nayar, in his report to the President of India on Oct 5, 1993 recommending a proclamation of Article 356 stated that the conflict was an expansion of National Socialist Council of Nagalim [NSCN] (I)'s expansionist design, fight for control of NH-39 and Moreh for illegal resources borne out of smuggling of narcotics and contraband trade, and to get a major share of compensation of Rs. 12.5 crores of Maphou Dam in Thoubal. Further, he added that ethnic complexion has been injected by the leaders of both the communities to further their political agenda.[7] Views similar to that of V.K.

Nayar were also echoed by Kuki Students Organisation (KSO) and under ground outfits like Kuki National Front(KNF),Kuki Defence Force(KDF), and Kuki National Organisation(KNO) when they attributed the subversive activities of NSCN(IM) as responsible for the outbreak of the clashes. NSCN(IM) on the other hand maintains that the whole problem of Kuki-Naga conflict arises out of India Government's appeasement policy towards the Kukis and the demand for the creation of Kuki Homeland.[8]

The immediate cause as ascertained from both the affected Kuki and Naga residents of the Chandel District, was the antagonistic stand by the Nagas and the Kukis over the recruitment of teachers for Chandel Autonomous District Council (CADC) scheduled to be held on 5 September, 1992. A day before the DPC was to be held, the Kuki Students Organisation Chandel called a bandh at the District. Some violent incidents took place at Ziontlang but not to the extent of killing. There was a tussle between Naga applicants who came for the interview and the Kuki youths.[9] There were also reports that the Naga militants also prevented Kuki candidates who came for the said DPC at Moreh side. It later assumed the form of Kuki-Naga hostilities after such incidents became more frequent.[10] According to Kuki Students' Organisation (KSO), Morung Makunga, Minister of State for Tribal Development was responsible for the outbreak of the Kuki-Naga turmoil. As per their version, the said DPC would have been conducted during TN Haokips' tenure, but it was not held following a request from Morung Makunga. But Morung Makunga after becoming Minister of state for TD called for the said DPC, which he himself told his predecessor that "it will not be held unless Sixth Schedule was implemented".[11]

The existence of village boundary disputes at places where Nagas and Kukis co-inhabited as neighbouring villages has also contributed in sustaining the clashes. Examples can be cited of Kangol Khunou,an affected Maring Village in Chandel which had boundary disputes with the neighbouring Kuki Village,Modenphai.[12] Likewise,in Senapati also,inter-village boundary disputes appeared between K.Moljol, an affected Kuki village, and Ngalan NagaVillage,[13] and Harup Kuki village with Harup Naga and Thonglang Naga Village,[14] Gelnel Kuki village with Kadi Anal village,[15] and T.Gojang of Saikul area also had boundary disputes with the neighbouring Naga village.[16] boundary disputes were also there between Lasan, an affected Kuki village of Tamenglong District and the neighbouring Naga village, Lamka.[17] Joupi, the erstwhile Kuki village under Tamei S.D. of Tamenglong district also had irreconcilable differences on various matters including the border disputes with the neighbouring Liangmai Naga village, Lenglong.

The influx of displaced population following eviction from their respective villages also acts as a catalyst in escalating the tension of the already grave imbroglio. Those displaced were a frustrated lot as they were evicted from their erstwhile villages and in most cases their properties were either confiscated or destroyed. They also brought with them the stories of inhuman atrocities and brutalities meted out to them by the contesting tribal groups. N. Hepuni Mao, Chairman of the Kangpokpi Naga Organisation, an organisation of Displaced Nagas from Kangpokpi has stated," Even though, already there were reports of Kuki-Naga ethnic flare up, we never imagined, it will ever affect the harmoniously co-existing Kukis and Nagas of Kangpokpi. But gradually, the situations became complex with the pouring in of Kuki refugees from other districts. They afterwards together with the Kuki locals directed their vengeance to the Naga residents of the area."

It is quite probable that the Kuki-Naga turmoil were further worsened by the prevailing political uncertainties at that time.The Naga and the Kuki Ministers were also not in good terms with each other as R.K. Dorendro, the Chief Minister of Manipur, during 1992-94 has said: "...there is a lot of pent up feelings amongst both the Naga and Kuki Ministers.[18] *The Indian Express*, in its editorial on Jan 3,1994 stated: "Central intervention was in fact widely expected when it becomes clear that faction ridden Dorendro Singh Ministry was thoroughly incompetent with either the bloody Kuki-Naga Ethnic Conflict..." "There were also reports that in his efforts to contain the Kuki-Naga clashes, he did not get full support from his cabinet colleagues who were waiting for an opportunity to let him down".[19]

The Governor of Manipur also had earlier expressed his displeasure at the inaction of the state government in his proposal to mobilise public opinion for defusing the tension between the Nagas and the Kukis. One major reason for the imposition of PR from January 1,1994 by placing the Assembly under animated suspension was the Government's failure to check the Kuki-Naga clash. However, there was no sign of improvement in the law and order situation arising out of Kuki-Naga clashes during that six month's time of the President's Rule. So, "the Parliament had approved the extension of President's Rule for another six months with the belief that the extension should give an opportunity to the Governor to restore normality without political interference."[20]

A careful scrutiny is needed to understand the role of the Indian Armed Forces in relation to the clashes. The Army did a good job by organising Kuki-Naga get togethers at some places. Such ventures were appreciated by both the Kukis and the Nagas as it happened at a time when they cannot even bore the sight of each other. But such goodwill were eclipsed by their alleged involvement in instigating one against the other. The Naga Patriotic Front in its press release on August 25, 1993 accused the Indian Army of having nexus with the Kukis. Hanglen, President of KNO in his interview in *The Hindu* stated that "The Kuki militants in Chandel have recieved moral and material support from various agencies of the Government of India."[21] The greatest casuality is the credibility of the Indian Security Forces who were alleged to have involved in instigating the one against the other.[22]

Women also bear the brunt of the arbitration by the armed forces arising out of armed conflict situation. Many women were sexually assaulted, tortured, and killed by the armed forces in Manipur. During 1993 to 1997, in the hill districts of Manipur, as many as five women were killed, another 25 were sexually assaulted including rape and many others received bullet injuries.[23]

It was during the period 1992-1996 that Kuki-Naga clash was at its worst. There were large-scale displacements. Academic pursuits particularly at the pre-matric level came to a complete halt for one to four years. Many had afterwards completely abandoned education. The livelihood options for them have become very limited. Because of the prevailing threat perception in their movement, they cannot pursue any economic activities. All their past savings were liquidated during the clashes. According to the United Naga Council (UNC), during the period 1992 to 1997, 677 persons were killed in all, out of which 207 were Nagas and the remaining were Kukis. Another 302 were also injured out of which 197 were Nagas. A total of 5452 houses were burned down during 1992 - 96, out of which 2581 belonged to the Nagas.[24]

The governmental machinery was also very insensitive in redressing the grievances of the affected people. Many affected villages are yet to receive their rehabilitative assistance from the Government. Many still didn't receive any *ex-gratia* for the unnatural death of their family members in relation to the clashes. The complacency of the Governmental machinery in addressing the grievances of the affected people can be understood from the fact that in the early 90's, an SDC of Tamei, Lithui Golmei, a Naga was killed while on official duty near one of the Kuki villages under Tamei S.D. and his family is yet to receive an ex-gratia for want of report from the Police Station concerned.[25] The mid-90's also saw the sudden increase of concrete buildings in the tribal pockets of the valley, particularly in Imphal. Whether it can be taken as a parameter for the assumption that money meant for the rehabilitation has not reached the affected people is worth considering and invites further study. Out of a total 687 killed in Manipur, only 150 have been given ex-gratia, the rest still remains unattended.[26]

The Kuki-Naga clashes expose that ethnic consideration has a greater hold than religion. The succeeding years of the clashes saw the dismantling of the Church as Aimols dissociated themselves from the Kom Rem Baptist Association and formed the Aimol Baptist Association.[27] The conflict also has led to a greater polarisation of vote-bank on ethnic lines. It was during Holkhomang Haokip's tenure as MP that Poumai was given recognition as Scheduled Tribes. But in the Lok Sabha election that was held shortly after their inclusion, he was not successful in translating their goodwill into potential votes.[28] The Kuki leaders and Activist Organisations in their attempt to delegitimise the claim of "Naga Inhabited Areas" quoted the statistics of the votes secured by the Kuki candidates in the Assembly and Parliamentary elections as if there exist ed no cross- voting across ethnic lines. During the clashes, the Government had a policy of opening ethnically homogenous grouping centres as they cannot provide security cover in all the villages. This has resulted in expansion of the villages.

The smaller intermediary tribes also have their share of anxieties and traumas as they were caught in between the devil and the deep sea. There were reports from some Kom and Aimol villages that there were pressures from both the Kuki militants and the Naga militants, so as to assimilate them in their respective fold.[29] It might be because of such big fish eating the small fish kind of situation that some tribes from among the old Kuki groups like, Lamkang and Maring have called themselves as Nagas. The clashes were not only confined to the five hill districts of Manipur but it also spread out to Thoubal, Bishnupur and even Imphal. Lalkholen Thangeo, Vice President of Kuki Inpi who came to attend Peace Meeting held at Manipur Baptist Convention (MBC), Imphal on 8 October, 1995 was abducted by suspected Naga Militants from Khuman Lampak bus parking and later found killed.[30] Sensing troubles, the District Magistrate had much in advance placed Nagaram and Zomi villa Area of Imphal under CrPC- 144 on 16 April 1993.[31] There was also newspaper report of raiding Naga residence in Imphal by unknown armed forces[32] and attempt of kidnapping a Kuki girl by unknown Naga youths.[33] Fortunately, despite such stray incidents, Imphal continued to remain least threatened by the clashes. Otherwise, the complexities of the clashes would have assumed mammoth proportion, and, they, the Kukis and the Nagas would have been left with lesser alternatives for taking refuge and shelter.

The Kuki-Naga clashes also sow the seeds of the Kuki-Paite clash. Many of the displaced Thadou Kukis came for cover and were accommodated at Churachandpur. This has created a fear among the other constitutent tribes of Kuki-Chin groups, like Paite, Simte and Tedim-chin that they will be out-numbered by them. Law and order problems relating to flesh trades, extortion and burglary were on the rise as those displaced came to Churachandpur in a pauperised state.[34] So, heavy population influx of Thadou Kukis, activities of Kuki insurgents coming from Sadar hills side who didn't have any knowledge of the local sentiment coupled with the confrontationist attitude of the Paite militants proved to be fertile grounds for the outbreak of the Kuki-Paite clashes.[35] The Kuki militants' endeavour for retaining the Paite,

Vaipheis, Simte, Zou, Tedim-Chin and Mate ended with a compromise between Kuki Inpi and Zomi Council by agreeing to mutually respect the Kuki and Zomi nomenclature and left it to individual choice.[36] In the case of the Nagas, "Identification with the Nagas has been a process of Pan-Naga identity."[37] The identity of the evolving Naga nationality is still at the abstract level. So, the problems might arise on the question of whom to exclude and include when the process of concretising Naga identity comes up. As "the Nagaisation process was greatly strengthened by the Naga insurgency[38] the dissentors, who prefer to maintain their distinct identities by not affiliating to either of them, must have been silenced by the language of violence.

Also, the Kuki-Karbi clashes in Assam during 2003 to 2004 should not be viewed in isolation with the Kuki-Naga clashes. There were allegations by the Karbi militant outfit, United Peoples' Democratic Solidarity (UPDS), that Karbies would be outnumbered by the Kukis in Karbianglong due to a Kuki influx since Kuki-Naga clashes occurred in adjoining Nagaland and Manipur in 1992.[39]

The casualties of the Kuki-Naga clashes show a downward trend since 1997. But the vulnerability of resurfacing the clashes at any time continues to persist. Till date, there have been reports that the Naga militants are still collecting taxes from the Kuki villages and the Kuki militants from the Naga villages. In some interior areas of Churachandpur, the Naga militants had, since the late 90s prohibited the Kuki locals from assessing forest resources, saying that those forestlands belong to Nagalim.[40] In a report appeared at the local daily, *The Sangai Express*, on 11September 2004, the Kuki outfit, Kuki Liberation Army (KLA) demanded a clarification from the NSCN(IM) on whether extortion notices have been served to chiefs of Kuki villages situated at Senapati and Thoubal districts and urged the latter to withdraw the extortion notes as it has the potential to renew the Naga-Kuki conflict. Entering into cease-fire with the ethnic army is no doubt a positive step by the state. But the failure of the state machinery to monitor and control the abuse and misuse of the cease-fire ground rules would certainly have immediate and long-term consequences in the inter-group relations among the various ethnos of the North-east.

In the meantime, many new Naga villages have come up at the site of the former Kuki villages and Kukis also have established new ones at the site of abandoned Naga village. For example newly established Naga villages, namely Dikuiram, Kawalong, Puilong and Kabonram were established at the site of the erstwhile Kuki villages, namely lower Zampi, Dulen, Buning and Toloulong respectively all at Tamei Sub-Division of Tamenglong District.[41] Likewise, at Saikul area of Senapati District, a new Kuki village, Saijang, has come up at the site of erstwhile Naga village, Makeng.[42] But, quite ironically, most of these newly established villages are now recognised as revenue villages.

Time is no doubt a great healer. But Kuki-Naga tension is too complex a problem to keep on hoping naively that time will ameliorate their strained relationships. The MBC also formed a Peace Committee on 17 September, 1992. But all their peace efforts were in vain.[43] The All Manipur Tribal Goodwill Mission formed under the Chairmanship of Mr. A.S. Arthur, Ex-MLA, with 35 eminent social workers, representing all hill districts proved to be a damp squib and no longer heard afterwards following the arrest of its mission Chairman by the Government Authority for keeping unlicensed fire arms.[44] Among other efforts for restoring peace and normalcy, mention may be made of Committee for Peace and Integrity (COFPAI) formed by 48 voluntary organisations of Manipur, including United Naga Council (UNC) and, Kuki Inpi Manipur (KIM) under the initiative of All Manipur United Clubs' Organisation (AMUCO) and

National Reasearch Centre (NRC).[45] For four months COFPAI, surveyed all the hilly areas of Manipur to understand peoples' aspirations and 654 in camera meetings were also held at different places during that period emphasising peaceful co-existence and fraternal ties of brotherhood.[46] COFPAI concluded their campaign on May 3, 1995, (the formal closing day) though AMUCO and NRC continued to work rigorously for promoting peaceful co-existence and for strengthening fraternal ties of brotherhood, till date.

Committee for Restoration of Normalcy (CRN) which was formed by the apex bodies of both the Kukis and the Nagas, KIM and UNC, with the objective of mediating the tension and addressing the grievances arising out of tension also came to an abrupt end following UNC's resolution for demanding inclusion of Manipur in the Indo-Naga Ceasefire on 22nd August, 1997. Because of it KIM withdrew itself from CRN on 2nd September 1997 terming the said UNC's resolution as a Second Quit Notice to the Kukis.[47] It will be near impossible task to resurrect such committees like COPFAI and CRN constitutive of both the Kukis and the Nagas, as militant outfits of the Ethnic groups concerned might come in between. Civil societies who can be independent critiques of both the non-state and the state actors were and are found wanting. The process of militarising civil society by the ethnic armies is still rampant. The latest example being the issuing of diktats through local newspaper to the Kuki Inpi regarding the election of its new office bearer by the Kuki National Council (KNC), the umbrella organisation of KNF (T. Samuel), KNF (St.Thangboi), KRA, and United Kuki Liberaion Front (UKLF)[48] So, the options of seeking solutions through intervention by civil societies as upholders of civic virtues is still very opaque.

India's past history of partition still has relevance with the communal violence in the country. But unfortunately, some organisations are advocating another partition in this

North Eastern part of the country, with malicious propaganda towards the other communities. Examples can be cited of one such propaganda by the UNC. "On many occasions, the Meiteis have played divide and rule policy amongst the tribals by instigating one against the other. The issue of Sadar Hills which is meant to carve out a district for the Kukis out of the Naga areas, is a unique case. The Naga-Kuki clash has the direct hand and instigation of the Meitei politicians and valley based insurgents"[49] Such irresponsible statements can also narrow the scope of involving the majority communities in resolving the conflict as impartial mediators.

It is also significant to note that in some areas where Kukis and Nagas were cohabited, after getting displaced for sometime, the locally evolved conflict resolution models agreed mutually by both the parties have enabled them to return to their former site and co-exist in a state of normalcy. Usually, in such models, they mutually agree not to provide information on operative intelligence and strategic importance of their neighbouring village to the militants belonging to their ethnic group or any; and in the case of any abduction of Kuki civilians by the Naga militants, the neighbouring Naga villages will take risk and responsibility for the safe release of the abductees, likewise, by the neighbouring Kuki villages in the case of abduction of Naga civilians by Kuki militants.[50] Such models were found to be quite effective. People to people exchanges across ethnic lines as initiated by various organisations have also the potential of bringing amity through inter-personal relation, as they can unwind the stereotype harboured by them about each other.

As ethnic assertion has already started, nobody would want to shed the identity of its racial group. Moreover, the Bolshevik Revolution of erstwhile Soviet Union and the Communist movement in China were able to achieve success only after injecting a heavy dose of patriotism, which is in contradiction with their objective of striving for Stateless society. So, seeking "Socialist solution[51] as desired by some political leaders of Manipur doesn't seem to promise any emancipative potential as ethnic consideration are here to stay and replacing it by class consciousness sounds too utopian. As such, it will be better to find ways of accommodating ethnic nationalism in the larger canvas of plural democracy.

However, the public burial of the Kuki-Naga clash is still not within sight. Performing the last rites of the Kuki-Naga clashes with mutual agreement by both the Kuki and the Nagas will not be possible until and unless the affected displaced populace of either groups are allowed to return and settle at their erstwhile villages and former sites. But such a vision is also blurred by the lack of commitment on the part of the government and civil societies and partisan design of the insurgent groups.

NOTES

1. Gopal Krishnan, R.1995. *Insurgent North Eastern Region of India.* New Delhi: Vikas Publishing House, p.91.
2. *Ibid.*, p.92
3. *Ibid.*, p. 92,93
4. Haokip, P.S. *Kuki and the Naga Public Clash.*
5. "An Exclusive interview with Rishang Keishing", *The Freedom*, (Local Daily), May 24, 1993, Imphal.
6. "Dorendro's Last Interview", *The Freedom* (Local Daily) 2 January, 1994, Imphal.
7. "Historic Report of Manipur – To Secretary to the President of India", in *The Freedom* (Local Daily), Imphal March 8 to 10, 1994
8. Sumi, V., and K. Timothy., K.,(not dated) "*Cry for Justice*". MIP, GPRN Publications.
9. Thangboi (Pseu), December 6, 2004, *Interview by the Author*, at Sita, Chandel.

10. K. Mopham, March 30,2004, *interview by the Author*, at Pallel, Chandel.
11. May 1, 1993, *"Imphal-Moreh Blockade is the Handwork of Morung Makunga*" appeared in The Freedom (Local English Daily).
12. Yamthing, March 18, 2004, *Interview by the Author*, at Chandel.
13. Kaikholal Kipgen, Chairman(V/A) March 1,2004, *Interview by the Author*, at K. Moljol, Senapati.
14. Seilam Haokip, March 23, 2004, *Interview by the Author*, at Kangpokpi.Senapati.
15. James (Pseu), April 3,2004, *Interview by the Author*, at T. Waichong, Senapati.
16. Thongkhulen, February 10, 2004, *Interview by the Author*, at T.Gojang,Senapati.
17. Laminlung, March 23, 2004, *Interview by the Author*, at Kangpokpi IT Road Junction, Senapati.
18. Jan 1, 1994, "Dorendra's Last Interview", in *The Freedom* (Local English Daily).
19. January 6, 1994 in Editorial of *The Hindu*, Madras.
20. May 13, 1994 in Editorial of *The Hindu*, Madras.
21. March 24, 1991 in *The Hindu*, New Delhi.
22. G. Kamei, 1994 in "The Naga-Kuki Ethnic Conflict", *Souvenir of AIMSFED 3rd Annual Conference cum Literary Meet*. p. 21.
23. *Statement of the Joint Forum of Indigenous Women (North East India) South National Conference of Women's Movement* ,December1997,Ranchi,Pp28-30.
24. UNC, Manipur, 1998, "*A Brief Report of the UNC, Manipur for the year 1995-1998*", Manipur, UNC. P.44, 45.
25. Th. Kiran, S.D.O, Tamei, August 11, 2004, *Interview by the Author*, Tamei.
26. Gangte, P., "*Human Rights Violation in Hill Areas*", TIPS, in Human Rights Review, Imphal: TIPS, 2002, p.19.
27. Alok Aimol,T., and Khamnu., L.D., October 4, 2003 *Interview by the Author*, at Louchilbung Aimol Village, Churachandpur.
28. Ngupani, N.G. (Field Investigator, CSDS, National Election

Study 2004) March 23, 2004. *Interview by the Author*, at Senapati.

29. Interviewees' Name and Place withheld, October 4, 2003. *Interview by the author*
30. Haokip, P.S., *Kuki-Naga Public Clash.*
31. "Ethnic Violence Reaching the Heart of Imphal", in *The Freedom,* Imphal, April 18,1993
32. *The Freedom,* Imphal May 24, 1993.
33. *The Freedom,* Imphal, November 6, 1994 .
34. Touthang, S., February 20, 2003. *Interview by the Author*, Imphal.
35. Khongsai, Lungsa, November 1, 2003. *Interview by the Author*, at Maulson, Churachandpur.
36. "Peace Returns in Churachandpur", *The Freedom*, October 2,1998
37. Kamei, G., 1997, "Crisis of Identity in Manipur", *Philosophy of History and Historiography of Manipur*. MURC Publications, p.149.
38. *Ibid.*
39. Parveen Kumar, *"Karbi-Kuki Clashes in Assam"* in K. Santhanam (ed.), *Strategic Analysis*, Apr-June 2004, Vol.28. No.2, New Delhi: The Institute for Defence Studies and Analysis.
40. Interviewees' Name and place withheld. October 17, 2003
41. Rengbao (Pseu) Employee SDO, Tamei, August 9, 2004, *Interview by the Author,* at Tamei, Tamenglong
42. Lalhong, Village Chief, February 9, 2004, "*Interview by the Author*" at Saijang, Saikul.
43. KNC A Genocide in Manipur, p. 4,5.
44. *Ibid*, p.5.
45. COFPAI pamphlet, not dated.
46. *Souvenir, Manipur Integrity Day*, August 4, 2004, AMUCO, Imphal.
47. "CRN No Longer Exist", in *The Freedom*, Imphal , September 3, 1997
48. *The Sangai Express*, September 30, 2004.

49. UNC, December 10, 2002 "*Issues Relating to the Territorial Integrity of Manipur-At Naga Perspective*", UNC Working Group ,p.36
50. Mousinpha, T.K. (D.I. District Council), 2 May 2004 *Interview by the Author*, at Chandel.
51. Poknapham, 1994, (Sp.Ed) "*Manipurgi Chingda Kanglupki Irang*", Imphal, Poknapham.

5

Socio-Political Relation Between the Moirangs and the Ningthoujas during Historical Period

— M. Ranjana

According to the topographical position Manipur is divided into two parts, i.e. plain and hill area. The hill people are of two ethnic groups i.e. Nagas and Kukis and the valley was inhabited by different ethnic groups. But these people in later period were known as Meiteis. There were seven principalities in the valley area. At a particular stage of time all of them had enjoyed the independent status. Later on, they were assimilated to the social and cultural fabric of the Ningthouja clan.

The Ningthouja clan was established in the first century A.D. under the leadership of Nongda Lairen Pakhangba[1]. Gradually all the other ethnic principalities were assimilated to one after another. In course of time Angoms , Kha-Nganba, Sarang Leishangthem were merged to the Ningthoujas. The Luwangs and the Khumans were also absorbed by the Ningthoujas. Only the Moirangs and the Ningthoujas were remained as a powerful ethnic group in the valley area till 14th Century AD. The Moirangs were defeated by the powerful Ningthouja king in 1432.[2] Though the Moirangs were defeated they enjoyed the status of an autonomous principality up to 18th century.[3]

The main objective of the paper is to make a humble attempt to analyse the socio-political relationship between Moirangs and the Ningthoujas which is still not properly explore. Due to the absence of archeological evidences, I have depended entirely on the available literary sources.

The scholars and writers of the ancient period had an impression that the Moirangs and the Ningthoujas were originated from a single divine personality. On the basis of this mythical account they make an attempt to give a concept of same legendary origin and reflected it in the preparation of genealogy and chronicles.[4] Whereas, the modern scholars propounded a new theory rejecting the legendary origin of these two ethnic groups. According to them they came to Manipur from different place and direction.[5]

The relationship between the Moirangs and the Ninghtoujas developed from the very beginning. Old literary texts like *Numit Kappa* and *Chakpa Khunda Khunthak* recorded that Numit Sana Khomdon later known as Pakhangba fled to Moirang and settled here for many years after his defeat in the hands of Khwai Nungjengba Peba, the leader of Khaba clan. He was warmly received by the chief of Moirang when Pahangba was at Moirang, he had two sons Mungyang Chaoba and Tangru Lumiba. Their descendents were later known as Mungyangjam and Lairenjam and entered into the Moirang Khuwang Salai, a sub-clan of Moirang. Pakhangba received the support of the Moirangs and able to defeat the Khabas completely.[6] Not only this Khujoi Tompok, the son of Nongda Lairen Pakhangba, the founder of the Ningthouja dynasty, was also captured the throne with the support of the Moirang, Luwang and Angom.[7]

Apart from this friendly relationship, the Ningthoujas and the Moirangs also had matrimonial alliance. The daughter of Ura Konthouba , the Ningthouja king was married to Puriklai Lai Phacheng, the Moirang and Naothingkhong the Ningthouja king married the daughter of Puriklai Sana Rakhwa while he was staying at Khuman principality for education. Meidingngu Thangbi Lanthaba of Ningthouja married the only daughter of Puriklai Chingkhu Telheiba of Moirang. Songlen Lanthaba, the Moirang king married the daughter Meidingngu Khumomba. Thus,Maharaja Garibniwaza and his son Shyamsai married the Moirang princess.[8]

Beside this friendship with matrimonial alliance they also helped each other at the time of war. During the reign of Moirang king Songlen Lanthaba, the Kabaws invaded Ikop, a village within the principality of Khuman. The Khumans felt they would not be able to resist the invading forces and also they requested both the kings of Moirang and Ningthouja for help. The two kings sent their forces to assist the Khumans against the Kabows.[9]

However, there were many evidences about the internal conflict between the Ningthoujas and the Moirangs. Some of such conflict led to open war. According to Cheitharol Kumbaba, the Ningthouja royal chronicle, it is said that during the reign of Khongtekcha (763-773) the Moirangs invaded within the territory of the Ningthoujas but they were defeated [10]. After this event a series of fights were continued between the two ethnic communities for a quite long time. During the reign of Moirang king Chingkhu Telheiba a battle was fought with the king Thangbi Lanthaba.[11] After this battle enmity between the two communities was revived. But the expansionist policy of the Moirang king Sanahongba was not acceptable to Ningthouja group and so it was challenged by Punshiba. He invaded Moirang and a battle was fought at Saibung. The Ningthoujas though won the battle, their king Punshiba was wounded severely and succumbed to the injuries. Therefore, the remaining part of the war was led by his son Ningthoukhomba and occupied Moirang.[12] After this battle, equal status of Moirang with the Ningthoujas came to an end and Moirang reduced to the status of dependent principality. According to G. Kabui 'the status of Moirang was an autonomous principality'.[13] The Ningthoujas took the role of King maker of Moirang. After the death of Sanahongba, all chiefs of Moirang were appointed by the Ningthoujas among the princes of Moirang who were at Kangla. After AD1432, some princes of Moirang with other royal members began to settle at Imphal. They never tried to go back to Moirnag. Instead, they joined the court of Ningthoujas as court nobles and helped them in the administration. During the reign of Kyamba, the son and successor of Ninthoukhomba, the Moirangs became a good friend of Ningthoujas. When he attacked Mongkhwang he suffer a lot in the battle, but he was rescued and protection was given by Namba Saraba, a grandson of Sanahongba the last independent king of Moirang. In recognition of his help, King Kyamba appointed him as the leader of Naharup Pana,[14] even though it was not institutional but attached to the powers and function of the king or delegated to a person or others with the status of a noble or of an appointed person of the king. Thus after having as experience of long enmity between the two principalities a friendly relationship was again revived. Sometimes, the Ningthouja kings appointed the chief of Moirang to the post of Nongthonba. Originally, this post was created by the Ningthoujas to look after the affairs of South-Western side of Manipur valley. Thus, the Moirang chief by having the position of Nongthonba had administered Moirang with the help of three other nobles such as Nairel Hishaba and Phamthakcha.[15]

When the Ningthoujas became weak during the last half of the eighteen century, the Moirangs under the leadership of Khellemba became king of Manipur with the help of the Burmese. And Moirang became the centre of administration.

He introduced many changes in the administration of Moirang. He created the post of Mantri, Pukhramba, Nongthomba, Ahallup Lakpa, Naharup Lakpa, Khabam Lakpa, Laipham Lakpa, etc., as the Ningthoujas for Moirang.[16]

Society

From the very beginning both the Moirangs and the Ningthoujas had kinship and lineage based social system. The smallest unit in the society was a family where the father dominated and controlled all the family affairs. Thus the society was a patriarchal society. The descendants of the father formed a lineage than a clan. The clan is the foundation of their social formation. In the society of both communities patrilineal descent was the most important structural feature. Both communities were exogamous and had strict marriage system. Among the Moirangs and the Ningthoujas cross cousin marriage system existed and it was very popular. In both societies divorce was not known. Once married there was no question of divorce. Widows were allowed to remarry again.

In religious belief also there were many similarities between these two ethnic communities. Both communities believed in ancestor worship. Among the Moirangs Lord Thangjing was regarded as their ancestor[17] and Lord Pakhangba among the Ningthoujas[18]. Above this, the people of both communities had worshipped many similar deities like Sanamahi, Nongshaba, Maharaba, Thangjing, Marjing, Khanachaoba, etc. Though, Thangjing was regarded by the Moirangs as their ancestor, the Ningthoujas worshipped Thangjing along with Marjing and Khanachaoba as tutelary deities.[19]

Both the Moirangs and the Ningthoujas worshipped Lord Sanamahi as household deity. Among the household deities Lord Sanamahi was one of the important deity and occupied a place of religious importance. Some scholars opined that Sanamahi was originated to Moirang and was spread to the

Ningthoujas in later period. In Moirang, Sanamahi was worshipped as lineage deity and placed next to Thangjing during their Lai-haraoba festival.

Not only this, the deity of Lord Nongshaba was also worshipped by both communities. To the Moirangs, Nongshaba was worshipped as lineage deity and regarded as the father of Lord Thangjing[21]. Whereas, the Ningthoujas began to worship Lord Nongshaba from the time of king Khagemba (1597-1652) by dedicating a shrine to Him at Kangla, the capital of Ningthouja kingdom[22]. To them, He was important as Lord Sanamahi and Pakhangba and prayed Him during cheiraoba by offering seasonal fruits and flowers[23].

Some of the rituals were also performed by the people of both communities. One of the best example is the ritual 'Lamtaiba'. The lamtaiba is a ritual in which the human beings requested to the concern deity of an area to protect them from the evil spirit and other unwanted elements. This ritual is done by Maibas or priest in the name of the king for the welfare of the kingdom and his people on the first Saturday of Meitei month Lamda (Feb./March)[24]. The Moirangs from the very beginning believed that they were different from the Ningthoujas, though they entered within the fold of Meitei society. They performed this ritual for their own at four different places of their ancient political jurisdiction i.e. at Huiyanpung, Nungchenpan, Hao-on-pat and Kumdampung. At these four places, they prayed Santhong Laining thou or Moriya Maiba, Marjing, Wangbren or Kayaba and Koubru[25]. Whereas the Ningthoujas also performed this ritual at four different places of their former jurisdiction i.e. at Kangla, Kakwa, Khurairung and Khwai Wangthonbi. The deities which they prayed are also different. They are Lammaba, Tumaba, Lamsenba, Tusemba, Hanba Kokchao, Hanba Leikham, Thinbi Lairenjamba and Itu Hanba[26]. Beside the rituals, the festival of Lai Haraoba was also performed by both communities. Though the Moirangs claimed that they performed this festival from the very ancient period of time, Lai haraoba was originated in its initial stage to the Khabas in Pre-Pakhangba time. The tradition of the Khabas was then followed by the successive rulers of the Ningthoujas. It was perhaps further developed, systematised and finally standardised in due course of time. This standardised haraoba was then adopted by the other clans or tribes.

About the festival of Lai haraoba, there were many points of similarity between Moirangs and the Ningthoujas in myth and day to day rituals. Most of the Meitei literary texts give opinions that the Moirangs followed the tradition of the Ningthoujas. Even the dance movement of the Moirang Lai haraoba was originated to the Ningthoujas.

After A.D 1432. the Moirangs became a section of Ningthouja population and from that time they began to identify socially and culturally with the Ningthoujas.

NOTES

1. Gangmumei Kamei, *Ancient History of Manipur,* Vol. I, p.91.
2. *Ibid.*pp. 148, 150, 164.
3. M. Ranjana, *The Moirangs : A Political History*, unpublished Thesis, p. 76.
4. *Thiren Meiram Liba,* ed. By N. Ibochouba, p. 21.
   - *Apokpa Thounirol,* MSS.
   - *Sagei Salairol,* ed. By L. Kalachand, pp. 139, 143.
   - *Puwari Khabi Thiren Thounirol,* ed. by Sh. Rajmohan, pp. 102-103.
   - *Emoinu Ahongbi Tungnapham,* ed. by Y. Budhichandra and Sanamacha pp. 35-42.
   - Meihourol Lathupa. Mss.
5. T.C. Hodson, *The Meitheir.* p. 6.
6. *Numit Kappa,* ed. by O.Bhogeshwar Singh, p. 26.
7. *Ningthourol Sheireng,* ed. by O. Bhogeshwar, p. 185. Ningthourol Lambuba, ed. by O.Bhogeshwar, pp. 17-21.

8. *Moirang Ningthourol Lambuba,* ed. by O. Bhogeshwar, pp. 50, 108, 176.
   - *Naothingkhong Phambal Kaba,* ed. by N. Khelchandra, p. 46.
   - *Cheitharol Kumbaba,* ed. by N. Khelchandra & L. Ibungohal pp. 79-80.
9. *Moirang Ningthourol Lambuba, op.cit.* pp. 200-205.
10. *Cheitharol Kumbaba,* p. 7.
11. *Ibid,* p. 16.
12. M. Ranjana, *op.cit.* pp.76-77.
13. G. Kabui. *op.cit.* pp.188-189.
14. *Moirang Ningthourol Lambuba* Vol:II ed. by O.Bhogeshwar Singh, p.84.
15. M. Narendra, *Moirang Kangleirol Amasung Manipur Itihaski Mari,* presented at the Archives Week org. by Manipur State Archives. 1995.
16. M. Ranjana, *op.cit.* p.154.
17. *Ibid,* p. 110.
18. S.N.Paratt, *Religion of Manipur,* pp. 10, 15.
19. *Ibid.* pp. 27, 28.
    M.Ranjana, *op.cit.* p.111.
20. W. Ibohal, *Early History of Manipur.*
21. S.N.Parratt, *op.cit.* p.15.
22. *Cheitharol Kumbaba,* p.38.
23. S.N. Parratt. p. 15.
24. M.Ranjana *op.cit.* p. 122.
25. *Ibid.* p.123.
26. *Umang Lai Khunda,* a quarterly journal published by All Manipur Umang Lai Khunda Committee, 9/10 issue p.22.

6

Ethnicity and Ethnic Fragmentation: The Question of Bishnupriya

— M. C. Arun

In the colonial and post-colonial period, ethnic relations in Northeast India have changed enormously. The ethnic groups in almost all the states have undergone various kinds of ethnic processes. Some ethnic groups amalgamate with one another, under one or other circumstances, to form a new identity. Some other ethnic groups have fragmented into new ethnic groupings. These ethnic processes are ethnic amalgamation in some cases and ethnic fragmentation in others. There are historical as well as sociological reasons to the emergent scenario of changing identities and ethnic processes.

The nature of ethnic amalgamation, in the post-colonial period, that took place in the North East India, is qualitatively different from that of the pre-colonial period. The long contact among the ethnic groups in an ecological niche and their interdependence for socio-economic needs were the main forces for the ethnic amalgamation. It was rather a natural process in those days. In the post-colonial situation, the amalgamation took place out of the political necessity or political bargaining of the ethnic groups. The equation of the ethnic amalgamations becomes more complex and goes beyond the natural course. On the other hand, ethnic fragmentation is observed in the region as a new phenomenon in the post-colonial period. Many ethnic groups that had been shaped in different historical bloc become disintegrated in the new historical conditions. The power relations between the different social groups within same ethnic group a become center of various controversies and conflicts. The interest of the groups play vital role in the disintegration of the ethnic group and emergences of new identities out of a single political identity. It was mainly due to the clashes of different interests of different groups. The Colonialism that disturbed the continuity of the power relations in these ethnic groups sowed the seed of the fragmentation. Today the region suffers the agonies of the division of its peoples.

Primordialist Explanation

In these ethnic processes, the ideology and politics of the ethnic groups are obviously expressed and translated into ethnic movements. What is the source of such feelings, ideology and movement? The source, according to the primordialists, is the primordial attachments. Shils, Geertz, started the primordialist explanations. Many anthropologists like Issacs, Stack, and Grosby followed this tradition. The main theoretical assumptions of this tradition are: (i) there is a primordial attachment, (ii) free from social interaction, but (iii) associated with an ineffable significance attributed to the tie of blood. The primordiality is thus linked with ethnobiology and the blood tie originated from a common ancestry.

The primordial explanation cannot fully be used in explaining and understanding the ethnic processes of northeast India. The primordiality of the ethnic groups does not operate in many cases. The myth of common ancestry and a tie of blood no longer hold the traditional ethnic boundaries. And neither can it explain the fragmentation of older ethnic identities.

One of the ethnic movements in Northeast India is the Manipuri fragmentation. The Bishnupriya-Meitei conflict in Assam and Tripura is a serious problem in Manipuri fragmentation. The Meiteis are mainly found in many places of Burma, Manipur, Assam, Tripura and Bangladesh. They and many other ethnic groups are collectively identified as the Manipuris. The Bishnupriya-Meitei conflict, however, is confined in the places of Tripura and Assam where the dominant group is the Bengali.

The Bishnupriyas had been living in the valley of Manipur under a central authority of Manipur. In spite of their different origin, racial affiliation and language, they had gradually become part and parcel of the Manipuri society. In due course of time, the Bishnupriyas identified themselves as one of the constituents of the Manipuri identity. The collective Manipuri identity was a result of long historical process of the ethnic melting pot theory. In this identity, the Meitei was the dominant group. Here one should note that the Meitei was not a homogeneous ethnic group. It was formed through a series of ethnic amalgamations. Many ethnic groups from different directions had come to Manipur at different points of time. They had been living there. Over a long period of time, they had been interacting for various socio-cultural and biological needs. Out of the interaction, they had evolved a new identity and polity.

The Bishnupriya was one of the constituent ethnic groups of the Manipuri identity. They came from an obscure place and settled in the southern part of Manipur valley. The primordial attachment of the Bishnupriya actors did not surface for many centuries. The blood-tie of the Bishnupriya was lost in the social intercourses in the valley of Manipur. They were subjectively and objectively Manipuri; one can even say that they were once identified as the Meitei.

The melting pot process in Manipur was first disturbed in the first quarter of 19th century. External forces seriously challenged the central authority of the state. Finally Manipur became subjugated under the Burmese (1819-1826) and later on an indirect British colony. The long historical process of melting pot was, thus, halted. Because of the heat of colonialism, the Manipuri identity suffered the threat of ethnic segmentation of various colours.

The primordialist explanation cannot explain the development of new identities out of the melting pot. Manipuri society is the collectivity where the primordial attachments of the ethnic groups had been melted down. In order to understand the ethnicity and ethnic fragmentation, we have to look for a new paradigm that will enable us to answer the question of ethnic formation, ethnic interests, ethnic fragmentation that took place during the colonial and post-colonial periods of the Third world.

Circumstantialist Explanation

Fredrik Barth, a student of Edmund Leach, took ethnicity as a type of social process in which the notions of cultural differences are communicated. Barth was influenced by Edmund Leach's *Political System of Highland Burma* (1954). According to Barth and other members of this school, the changing identities of ethnic actors are because of rational choice. The ecological, economic, political circumstances make it the instrument. So, ethnic group is rather self-ascription, subjective group.

A larger section of Bishnupriyas fled away from Manipur along with a good numbers of the Meiteis (including the **Pangal**) to Assam, Tripura and Bengal (specially the places, now in Bangladesh), at the wake of Burman occupation and atrocities in 1819. The Burmans installed puppet kings in Manipur and occupied the state for seven years. Out of fear of the tortures inflicted, many Manipuris fled westwards. The Burmans killed thousands of Manipuris and had decimated the population of the state to one-third. Those who fled away settled in various places in these foreign countries and had been living there for about one century. However, they had a strong sense of oneness with the Manipuri identity and had preserved the age-old traditions.

The Meiteis in foreign countries did not change their identity though their role model was the '*Bengali Bhadralok.*' Their language, religion, attitude were highly influenced by the dominant Bengali elements. But, their ethnic identity was unchanged because of an ineffable significance of the primordial attachment, not because of rational choice in a social interaction, as circumstantialists claim. Again the rational ethnic actors could not overcome the myth of blood-tie of the Meiteis.

The Manipuris of Surma valley formed together their first formal association, **Surma Valley Manipuri Society** (later changed its name to **Surma Valley Manipuri Association**) in 1934. The members included the Meiteis, the Bishnupriyas and the Pangals. But, just after the formation of the Association, the Meitei-Bishnupriya clash started in Cachar, Assam in the second quarter of 20th century. The state of Manipur and the **Nikhil Hindu Manipuri Mahasabha** (a formal Association in Manipur) tried to resolve the conflict in 1934. One could observe the feeling of the Manipuris in Manipur with the Resolution Number 4 of 30 May 1934 that read as: *That the* ***Nikhil Hindu Manipuri Mahasabha*** *feels its deep sense of sorrow at the recent bifurcation of the Meiteis and the Bishnupriyas of the Surma Valley; and it is hoped that such racial division does not exist in Manipur which is the original country of all the Meiteis. The Manipuris of the Surma Valley be requested to abandon this racial feeling, and the representations already submitted to their Government be corrected with deletions on the viewpoints of their racial bifurcation and animosity* (the translation is of Karam Manimohan Singh, as reproduced in his ***Hijam Irabot Singh and Political Movements in Manipur***, Delhi,

1989:50). Several attempts had been made from different quarters. But the attempts could not bring a permanent reconciliation. The gash became deeper and deeper. The Bishnupriyas asserted their linguistic identity but they like to be identified in association with the state from where they came to their present locations. They are subjectively Manipuri Bishnupriyas, a distinct group among the Manipuris.

The Meiteis of the Cachar District of Assam did not like Bishnupriya to be identified as Manipuri because (a) they speak a different language; (b) they are racially different. But, by doing so, the Meiteis deny (a) the Bishnupriya had been part and parcel of the state system and larger Manipuri (even the Meitei) identity; (b) they still have the Meitei clan organization; (c) they speak Manipuri language as second language, even in these foreign countries. The Meiteis of the Assam also have a fear that they would not get employment facilities and other opportunities given to the OBC by the Government of Assam. This fear is translated into the ethnic fragmentation. On the other hand, they feel sorry when non-Meitei language is recognized as Manipuri by AIR, state agencies including the educational curriculum. This state of mind is shaped by the Indian attitude to the ethnic identity as being associated with language. This division on the basis of language and recognition of linguistic communities as ethnic groups had been shaped and injected by the British and still they play a vital role in division of the peoples into several ethnic groups as colonial hangover.

The cleavage was due to the colonial policy prevailing in India that gave the division of the peoples along the linguistic line and is compounded by the economic interest of newly emerged middle class of the society. The politics of opportunists of both the Manipuri sections was evolved out of the unique historical experiences of the Manipuri in the colonial India.

The Bishnupriyas, though they speak a language akin to the Bengali, do not identify themselves as one of the Bengali ethnic groups. Is it because of their shared cultures with the Meiteis? One may note that the morphology of Bishnupriya language is similar to Bengali; while the structure of their language is deeply influenced by the Meitei grammar. In spite of common historical experiences and shared cultures, there is clash between the Meitei and the Bishnupriyas in Assam and Tripura today. Is it because of the Meitei chauvinism that denies the Manipuri identity to one of the lower caste in the traditional society? Or is it because of the ethnic relations between the Manipuri and the Bengali and within the Manipuri constituents? To answer these questions, one has to examine the historical processes of the colonial and post-colonial periods.

The cicumstantialist explanation fails to explain the process of ethnic segmentation. As the explanation is ahistorical by nature, it cannot explain the historical processes that took place in shaping and reshaping the ethnic identities. The ethnic realignment is not a question of interpersonal politics. It is not on the shoulder of individual rational actors, as presumed by the circumstantialists. The circumstantialists cannot explain the historical processes that go beyond the individual actors. We need to examine the power-relation prevailing in a particular historical bloc in order to understand the nature of ethnicity and ethnic processes.

National Question and Ethnic Problems

Ethnic base of power is becoming stronger in almost all the plural societies of the Third World. In Northeast India, too, the power game has had a paradigm shift. The power inside the state is in the hands of middle class, because the class formation in such peripheral capitalist society as the Manipuri society is not completed. It has the middle class as the 'upper' class. As an inherent quality of the structure of such a society, there is high competition among the individuals of the middle class.

The Bishnupriya-Meitei fragmentation is not seen in Manipur. In Assam, as both of them are ethnic minorities, competition among the social leaders of these minority communities is obvious. The competition is to gain more power in the power structure of their states. The leaders try to mobilize their bases on the basis of 'differences' that had been solidified in the process of melting pot and hence resulting in ethnic segmentation. The dynamics of segmentation attains its momentum over years and spreads the 'heat' to other places. Though the political agitations over the Meitei-Bishnupriya issues reach Manipur, so far, we do not see the ethnic cleavage in Manipur. The heat reached Tripura and some areas of Bangladesh.

The Bishnupriya leaders go beyond certain limit, of course, out of frustration in the competition, saying that they are the real Manipuri and that the Meiteis had driven them out. But, such propaganda provokes the 'people' and the power-base in their community is solidified. Likewise, neglecting the shared historical experiences, the Meitei leaders in Assam and Tripura also play the sentiment of the people by saying that the Bishnupriyas who were **Mayangs** once claim to be the 'original' Manipuri. Some leaders even go beyond limits and say that the Bishnupriyas are not Manipuri because their mother tongue is not Meiteilon. They forget that the test of the Manipuri nationhood is not the mother tongue. Thus, out of the middle class interests in power struggle, employment in government sectors, the Manipuri identity is reduced to a linguistic identity. The colonial division of Indian people into different linguistic group is extended to the Northeast India.

The linguistic division in Assam has to be considered in the analysis of Manipuri fragmentation in Assam and Tripura. The social fragmentation of the Assamese identity into various ethnic groups, the Ahom etc. has a parallelism. The linguistic consciousness of the Assamese middle class alienated lesser linguistic groups. The alienation is aggravated by the rise of ethnic middle class. So, Assam, since the last days of colonial rule, faces various ethnic assertions against the Assamese. The heat of alienation is inverted in case of the Manipuris in Assam. The majority Meitei was, in early twentieth century, educationally and politically inferior in 'foreign' countries; the minority Bishnupriya was superior in these aspects at that time. Though demographically and economically superior Meitei was superior in the Manipuri society, they were inferior in the state politics of Assam. Hence the social leaders of the Meitei in Surma valley did not like to share a common identity with the Bishnupriyas. With the passage of time, after the emergence of Meitei middle class and Bishnupriya middle class, the power axes of ethnic consciousness become more and more prominent.

Keeping the scene of ethnic fragmentation in the total national integrity of the Manipuris, we find that tho ethnic interests, arisen out of the middle class competition to get power, threaten the Manipuri nation. To get some political goals, some sectarian historians equate the Manipuri identity as that of the Meiteis. Their claims are fueled by the Meitei orthodox scholars who deny the post-Pamheiba historical realities and by the linguistic chauvinist scholars as well. Again these sectarian movements and scholarship are originated from the middle class competition to get more power in limited power structure of the peripheral capitalist society.

To get power in structure of the peripheral capitalist society, the middle class individuals can no longer use their kinship base. The individuals of well-to-do families in the pre-capitalist feudal (even in the colonial-feudal administration to a larger extent) used the kinship base as an effective instrument. In feudal Manipur, the kinship base was the primary source of power. The base has certain residue in the body politic but the feudal primary source of power is being replaced ethnic groupings, locality and class. As the peripheral capitalist society is maturing, the base no longer is useful. Hence, the ethnic base is used in the state power game. Thus, ethnicity in Manipur and Northeast India is question of power sharing among the middle class individuals. The competition is within the rules of game in the existing political system.

The ethnic fragmentation is thus within the framework of prevailing social and political system. It can be explained from two angles: (a) the nation building of India cannot touch this part of the country and its nationalism cannot operate in the body politic of this region; (b) the national integrity of the Manipuri nationhood disintegrate with the want of central authority and becomes segmented under the middle class pressure using ethnic sentiments. In short, India, like many other Third World countries, fails to develop a nation and a unified people. India is a state having different peoples and it cannot handle the plurality of its peoples. On the other hand, the power in a limited power structure in Northeast India blindfolds the middle class individuals in Manipuri society. Without questioning the entire power structure of larger system, the ethnic groups fight each other in a limited sphere of peripheral capitalist society.

7

The Kuki-Paite Clash (1997-98) in Manipur: A Study

— Senjam Mangi Singh

The Background

In Manipur, the 1990s witnessed a series of violent clashes involving different communities. First there was the outbreak of the Naga-Kuki clash in 1992 which continued till the late 1990s. This was followed by the May-riots (1993) involving the Meiteis and the Pangals (Manipuri muslims). The last in the series was the Kuki-Paite clashes in Churachandpur District of the state in 1997. Sparked off by the massacre of 24 June, 1997 in Saikul village, Churachandpur, it led to the killing of more than 400 people before the signing of a final peace accord by the involved parties on October 1998.

The Kuki-Paite clashes involved mainly two groups who were earlier grouped under the common nomenclature Kuki, – the Thadou speaking Kukis and the Paites. Before one proceeds further, it is important to elaborate a little bit on the issue of a common nomenclature among the tribes who were previously known as Kukis. At present, there are thirty-three scheduled tribes inside the state. Earlier, there were only twenty-nine. According to the classical classification of the earlier British ethnographers, of these 29 the Aimol, Anal, Chiru, Chothe, Gange, Hmar, Koirao, Maring, Koireng, Kom,

Lamkang, Monsang, Moyon, Mizo (Lushai), Paite, Purum, Ralte, Sukte, Simte, Thadou, Vaiphei and Zou are Kukis.[1] However, over the past 60 years or so, a number of terms have been advocated to be used as the nomenclature of these tribes and the quest for a commonly agreed upon nomenclature is still going on. In 1947, the term Khulmi (Khul = hole or cave, mi = man) was advocated on the ground that "Kuki" is an alien word whereas "Khul" is the common traditional place of origin of the tribes who were earlier grouped as Kukis.[2] The 1960s saw the popular use of the term Kuki-Chin to describe this group of people. Later, the word Mizo was added to it and by the beginning of the 1980s, the term Kuki-Chin-Mizo was widely used. In between, the mid 1970s also witnessed the demand for replacing all the other different nomenclatures by the word "Zomi". The word "Zomi" or "Zoumi" was intended to mean all the tribes who have been grouped under the term Kuki-Chin-Mizo. It came up as a protest against the words "Kuki" or "Chin", because the supporters of this term felt that they were all coined by outsiders.[3] For instance, the Paites, who are also the main supporters of the nomenclature Zomi, prefer the word "Zomi" to either "Kuki" or "Chin" because both are not indigenous words to them.[4] Locally and politically they call the country they inhabit "Zougam". Here, "Zou" means a hilly and cold place as opposed to a low lying hot area and "mi" means man. Hence, "Zoumi" means people of the hills or simply highlanders.[5] The supporters of this term are against the use of the term "Mizo" also because it wili amount to man-hill (Mi = man, Zou = hill) which is not proper.

Apart from the differences over a commonly acceptable nomenclature, a number of tribes of this group of people have also dissociated themselves from the group, and have either joined the Naga constellation or decided to assert themselves by their individual tribe-names. Some of them are also in a state of oscillation between the Naga and non-Naga groups of tribes. This has contributed a lot to the confusion regarding the question who were the Kukis at a given specific period of time, and there is the need for identifying those Kukis who were involved in the ethnic clashes of the 1990s.

Coming to that of the Kuki-Paite clashes in 1997, when the clashes took place, many of the tribes who were formerly grouped under the nomenclature Kuki have either joined the Naga constellation or have come to prefer to be known by their individual names or were found oscillating between the words Naga and Kuki. Of the remaining tribes also, opinions were divided. Some preferred to retain the term Kuki while others preferred the new term Zomi. Among the people of these tribes also, many accepted that both the term Kuki and Zomi refers to the same group of people and they preferred not to impose their preferences to their other fellow tribesmen. However there were also others who insisted on the acceptance of one particular term as the common nomenclature and wanted to impose the same to other people belonging to this group of tribes. Many of the Thadou speaking groups of people accepted the nomenclature "Kuki" and insisted on the acceptance of the same by their kindred tribes. The Paites, on the other hand, accepted the nomenclature "Zomi" but did not insist on the acceptance of it by their kindred tribes. Maintaining that the term Kuki and Zomi mean the same and refers to the same group of tribes, they wanted the individual tribes to be free to accept on their own either "Kuki" or "Zomi" as their group nomenclature. And the so-called Kuki-Paite clashes in Churachandpur during 1997 and early parts of 1998 were mainly between the Thadou speaking Kukis and the Paites. In the process, not only the Thadou-Kukis and Paites but people belonging to other tribes like the Zou, Simte, Vaiphei, etc. also became victims of the clashes.

Factors Responsible for the Clash

A number of factors have been responsible for the outbreak of the clash. During the late 1980s, one Kuki student was killed by his fellow Paite students at Nehru Marg, Churachandpur. The matter relating to the issue of compensation, however, was not amicably settled then.[6] One Paite group called "Om Pah Pah" which means something like immediate counter-action was also there when the killing took place. The group was also alleged as harbouring a tendency of isolating themselves from the Kukis.[7] The Kuki National Front (KNF) which was established in 1988 also collected taxes from the Paites and other tribes and those who did not pay the taxes were beaten up including the Paites.[8] The Paites also wanted to rename Churachandpur as Lamka. But the Thadou Kukis were not in favour of it. The Paite youths were also reported to have tainted colours on billboards which had the word Churachandpur on them during the night-time in and around the Churachandpur town.[9] In addition to this, Phungjathang and Hangkhalien, two former Paite MLAs from Churachandpur were also said to have lobbied for the Paite language to be used as the link language for a proposed station of the All India Radio at Churachandpur.[10]

Then, there was also the disagreement between the Thadou speaking Kukis and the Paites over the acceptance of the term to be used as the common nomenclature to describe all the Kuki-Chin-Mizo group of tribes in the state. The Thadou speaking Kukis were in favour of the term Kuki whereas the Paites favoured Zomi. The Paites claim that the only dispute between them and the Thadou Kukis is but acceptance of a comprehensive yet identical nomenclature.[11] They further claim that "In the event of such a dispute... the extremist underground faction of KNF(P) applied criminal force to induce the Zomi to acept the Kuki nomenclature propounding that the term Zomi is a misnomer . . . against the facts of history and their conviction."[12]

Another important factor which has contributed to the Kuki-Paite clash was the fact that the Kukis and Zomis incuding the Paites were at "loggerheads" over the issue of payment of Kuki Homeland taxes and fees. The Kuki insurgents, in the name of "Kuki Homeland" imposed (1) annual house tax at the rate of Rs.100 per family; (2) contribution of 10% of the total emolument of every government employee; (3) hefty road tax on buses and trucks; (4) special and emergency donation from well-to-do families and officials; (5) forest royalty; etc. etc. on all non-Naga tribes of Manipur.[13] The Zomi Re-unification Organisation (ZRO), an organisation patronised mostly by the Paites, Vaipheis, Zomi, Tedim Chins and Simtes[14] prohibited imposition and collection of such taxes from the Zomi group. The Kuki insurgents took this prohibition as a threat to their flourishing "exchequer" and challenge to their might.[15] Indeed, demand letters were reported to have been served to the residents of Saikul village of Churachandpur demanding Rs.100/- from every household on the eve of the June 24 massacre there in the village.[16] In addition to all these, the KNF(P) was also accused of making a series of armed attacks on Churachandpur with a view to control the populace and subjugate its economy and commercial turnover, and extort its share of revenue at its term and conditions to enhance its power.[17] So, when the Kukis wanted to control the Churachandpur market at their will, the whole communal clashes set in because of the resistance by other communities.[18] The Zomis described the taking away of money and of many valuable lives and properties of the Paites by the Kukis as the latter's "first line of attack" in their attempt to control Churachandpur.[19] In fact there were a series of attacks by the KNF(P) on the Paites before the massacre of June 24, 1997.

Extent of the Clash

Once the massacre of June 24, 1997 took place, violent clashes involving the Kukis and Paites spread like wildfire in many parts of Churachandpur District. Within the next couple of months or so, the KNF(P) was alleged to have kidnapped and brutally killed more than 100 Paite women and children, injured more than 50 innocent poor villagers and rendered more than 10,000 people homeles.[20] By October 22, 1997, as many as 123 cases of Zomi people killed and another 62 injured were there.[21] In addition to this, as many as 1465 Zomi houses were burnt down by November I[st] 1997 and another 32 school buildings, community halls, etc. belonging to the Zomis were also destroyed by August 1, 1997.[22] The overall extent of casualties suffered by both sides is yet to be established and authenticated. However, some 220 plus were killed before the end of September, 1998.[23] A government report also reported that a total of 4670 houses were burnt down during the clashes.[24] It is not a surprise then that during the clashes ammunitions became more essential than food for the people to survive.[25]

Steps Towards Reconcillation

One significant thing to be noted about the Kuki-Zomi people during the Kuki-Paite clashes was that most of their leading socio-cultural and political organisations came out immediately and condemned the clashes. More signficant was the fact that all the while they emphasised the basic unity and oneness of the Kuki-Zomi people without taking sides. This made the conflicting groups to ponder over the meaningless and futile nature of their clashes.

The first step towards finding a peaceful solution to the problem was taken up when the representatives of the KNF(P) and Zomi Revolutionary Army (ZRA) were brought together on July 7, 1997 to sort out all misunderstandings under the patronage of Pu C. Chawngkunga, Hon'ble Minister of Agriculture, Mizoram and four other MLAs from that state.[26] There were 30 signatories in the declaration which included one minister and four MLAs from Mizoram. Leading members of various Kuki/Zomi organisations like that of the KNF(P), Kuki National Organsiation (KNO), Kuki

National Army (KNA), Kuki Inpi (Churachandpur), ZRO, etc. were also there. As a result, both sides agreed the follwing with immediate effect:[27]

1. All forms of violence shall be shunned henceforth.
2. All improvised check gates and checking of vehicles shall be stopped forthwith.
3. Steps shall be taken for the displaced persons'/families' return to their respective places.
4. Free movement of all essential commodities shall be assured by the concerned parties.
5. Keeping in mind the principle of 'forgive and forget' nothing shall be done to violate the provisions of the agreement so as to ensure peace and tranquility between the two groups.

This agreement was immediately reaffirmed by the ZRO/ ZRA and the KNF(P) on the same day.[28] While re-affirming the agreement, the two sides further agreed to shun all offensive activities including kidnapping and obstruction or blocking of state and public highways with immediate effect.[29]

The clashes, however, continued unabatted and there were not less than 10 instances of violent clashes during the period from 7 to 20 July 1997, rendering the agreement utterly meaningless.

Another Cease-fire Agreement was signed between the KNF(P) and the ZRA on the initiative of Dr. Chaltonlien Amo, Hon'ble Minister of State (Medical) and the President, Hmar National Union, and his team. Under the Agreement, the KNF(P) and the ZRA agreed to cease all offensive activities including killing, kidnapping, burning of houses, wanton destruction of properties, extortion of money, threatening and intimidation of any kind, etc. for a period of 30 days from 11 August, 1997.[30]

Once again, the clashes continued unabatted and there were not less than 22 attacks during the period from August 11 to September 11, 1997, i.e. during the period of 30 days' Cease-fire between the KNF(P) and the ZRA as stipulated by the Cease-fire Agreement of August 11, 1997.

However, in the midst of all the frequent breaches of peace restoration norms, organisations like the Kuki Inpi, Kuki National Assembly, Kuki National Front (Military Council or MC), Zomi Council, Zomi National Volunteers, United Zomi Integration Council, etc. appealed to the fighting militants to shun violence and to accept the basic unity and oneness of the Kuki/Zomi people. All these brought tremendous pressure on the conflicting sides to find a peaceful solution to their differences. For a while, the possibility of the Kuki National Army joining the clashes was very much in the air with its warning on the Paites to either accept the Kuki nomenclature or face consequences.[31] But Kuki National Army later decided not to take sides in the clashes.

The state government also, for once, showed great political will to put an end to all the clashes and find a peaceful and lasting solution to it. While addressing an Inter-Church Pastors' Meeting at the State Guest House, the then Chief Minister Mr. Nipamacha said "It seems to be an open secret to the general public that some leaders of both the warring communities have been supporting the ethnic crisis using remote control devices".[32] Saying that the leaders of both the communities including ministers who were found encouraging the problem shall not be spared, the Chief Minister instructed his ministers who belong to the warring communities to take up every possible efforts to solve the problem as soon as possible.[33] The state government also constituted a High Level Committee headed by the Chief Minister with the Deputy Chief Minsiter as the Vice-Chairman. All the ministers and MLAs from Churachandpur Distict and two MPs of the state were also there in the committee as members. There were also representatives of the ZRO, Inter-Church Peace Committee, Kuki Inpi, Paite National Council and Hmar National Union. These steps were further followed by the signing of a Memorandum of Understanding by the Kuki Inpi, Churachandpur, on behalf of the KNF(MC), Kuki National Army, KNF(P) and Kuki Inpi Manipur, with the Zomi Council which was in turn authorized by the Zomi National Volunteers (ZNV), ZRO and ZRA to represent the Zomi as a whole in the event of peace talks with the Kuki Inpi, Churachandpur. In the Memorandum of Understanding signed on 26 March, 1998, the Zomi Council and the Kuki Inpi, Churachandpur, agreed to stop all forms of violence including burning of houses, kidnapping, killing, extortion, fabrication of rumours and even using harsh words against other communities.[34] It was also agreed that during the operation of this MOU, the leaders will resolve the differences between the two communities and sign a permanent peace accord. It also agreed that the two sides should jointly tour different parts of Churachandpur District to campaign for peace, and to convince the people to accept a permanent peace settlement. The ministers and MLAs belonging to the district were also decided to be urged to camp at Churachandpur from time to time.[35] Accordingly, the government launched a number of peace campaigns in different parts of Churachandpur like Tuibong and New Lamka. Ultimately, the final Peace Accord between the Zomis and Paites for restoration of peace and normalcy was signed on October 1, 1998. On the eve of signing the Accord, as a token of customary apology for mowing down the innocent persons and injuring other four persons on the night of the June 24, 1997, at Saikul village by the KNF thereby dragging the two communities into conflict, the Kuki Inpi offerd a feast by killing a four legged aninmal, a bull (Baurngtal), on September 29, 1998.[36] In response to the good gesture shown by the Kuki Inpi, the Zomi Council also killed another four-legged aninmal (Voktal) the following day which was happily shared together by the leaders of both communities.[37] Under the provisions of the Accord, it was agreed that "the nomenclature Kuki and Zomi shall be mutually respected by all Zomis and Kukis. Every individual or group shall be at liberty to call himself or themselves by any name, and the nomenclatures Kuki and Zomi shall not in any way be imposed upon any person or group against his/their will at any point of time."[38]

Some Observations on the Clash

Churachandpur is a district which is more or less exclusively inhabited by the group of tribes who were earlier described as the Kuki-Chin-Mizo group. However, over a period of time, the tribes have come to flaunt different nomenclatures. There are also many among the people who wants to be known by their individual tribe-name, and do not wish to be drawn under any particular nomenclature. Some tribes are also there who are oscillating between different nomenclatures. In such a situation, many Thadou speaking Kukis who got displaced from other hill districts of the state due to the Naga-Kuki clashes came to seek refuge and shelter in Churachandpur. It was also a time when the overall crime rate in general, and flesh trade in particular, was reported to be on the rise. Many saw a relation between this and the influx of displaced Thadou speaking Kukis in the district. It was in the context of such an environment that the Kuki-Paite clashes emerged.

The Kuki-Paite clashes also developed in the context of the quest for a commonly acceptable group nomenclature by a group of tribes claiming to have a common origin and close socio-cultural ties. Even though the clashes were popularly described as "Kuki-Paite" clashes, not all those tribes who were earlier known by the name Kuki were involved in the clashes with the Paite. It was only the Thadou speaking group of the people who were involved in the clashes with the Paites.

The Thadous, by and large, prefer the term Kuki, and during the Naga-Kuki clashes they became more and more synonymous with the word "Kuki". Hence the clashes got popularly termed as Kuki-Paite clashes. However, the clashes have also been variously described as "Kuki-Zomi Conflict"[39] "ethnic war between the Thadou-Kukis and the Paite-Zomis"[40] or simply as "family feud" between the Paites and Thadous.[41] This was because of the fact that the clashes developed in the context of accepting "Kuki" or "Zomi" nomenclature, and that the clashes were between the "Kuki" favouring Thadous and the "Zomi" favouring Paites.

It is also significant to note that the other tribes who favour the term Zomi, while showing solidarity with the Paites, emphasized all the time that the Kukis and Zomis are but one people, and reacted to the clashes with great restraint. All the while, many also appealed to the conflicting groups to settle their differences through peaceful negotiations. Among the supporters of the term Kuki also, there were many who accepted the futile and meaningless nature of the clashes and insisted that they are all one. For instance, the Kuki Inpi, the KNF(MC) and the Kuki National Assembly. The ready and willing acceptance by the common people that they are one irrespective of their differences over the term to be used as their nomenclature, proved to be too strong a binding force among them for the clashes to continue for long.

The Kuki-Paite clashes were also not an isolated event having no relation with the Naga-Kuki clashes. In fact it may be considered as a ramification of it. For instance, one finds the KNF(P) on its clarification for the clashes saying that Churachandpur is included in the proposed South Nagaland and that the ZRA has given shelter to the NSCN(IM).[42] The Kuki National Army, also urged the ZRA to stop supporting the NSCN(IM) and not to involve with the NSCN.[43] The ZRO, on its part, also contended that it was the Naga-Kuki clashes which induced the Kukis to feel the need for a homeland, and that this has subsequently contributed to the outbreak of the Kuki-Paite clashes. They also clarified the allegations of their having connections with the NSCN(IM) as false.

The Kuki-Paite clashes also reflected the friction-ridden state of the Kuki-Zomi people. They have numerous organisations, militant or otherwise. There are a number of organisations meant to be their common socio-cultural and political organisations. For example, the ZRO, UZIC, ZNV, ZDF, Kuki Inpi, Kuki National Assembly, KNO, Kuki National Volunteers, etc. Fortunately, most them have agreed among themselves that Kuki and Zomi refer to the same group of people and that they are one. However, the same cannot be said of the militant outfits among them, and there is no dearth of them. For instance, the KNF(P), KNF(MC), KDF, KNA, ZRA, etc. Unfortunately, some of them were not so accommodating towards one another. For example, the KNF(P) and the ZRA were at loggerheads. The Kuki National Army also gave serious warning to the Zomis to accept Kuki or face consequences. But the KNF(MC) did not join the clashes. In fact, the conflict which led to the clash was mainly between the two militant outfits-the KNF(P) and the ZRA. It was not between Kuki and Paite common peoples.

A number of other tribes who have favoured the Zomi nomenclature were also victims of the clashes. And it was not always in the hands of the Kukis. For example, there was the claim by the UZIC that 20 Zous, 12 Simtes, 9 Gangtes and 8 Vaipheis were killed and another 10144 people were rendered homeless by the ZRA (Paites).[44] What actually happened was that the smaller tribes, whenever they lived in proximity with either Kukis or Paites, were vulnerable to allegations of having sided with either of the two.

About the future, though most of the civilians had accepted the futility of the clashes, they are still not certain that the clashes will not surface again. Because, the ethnic militant groups involved in the clashes are still not disarmed. There also exist reports of some conflicts regarding control over land at Singhat side. The AIR, Churachandpur station also never got commissioned. As one Thangkhonlal Ngaite, Churachandpur, wrote: "The tribal patriotism is so great that many of them would prefer that the station is altogether buried instead of the link language going to a dialect other than their own"[45]

Finally, it may be said that the clashes tell a story of the difficult phases which a group of tribes claiming a common origin and close socio-cultural ties has to pass through before arriving at a commonly accepted nomenclature. It should serve as a grim reminder of the disastrous consequences of clashes among themselves while passing through such a crucial phase of their journey towards evolving a common national identity. Taken together in its totality, the entire episode also shows that demands for homeland and forcible collection of taxes in the name of it in areas characterised by ethnic plurality are not compatible with the realisation of peaceful co-existence and communal harmony. The successful intervention of the numerous civil organisations in solving the Kuki-Paite clashes also once again re-iterates the need for strengthening such organisations and enhancing their legitimacy to solve the problem of ethnic clashes.

NOTES

W. Nabakumar, "The Inter Ethnic Relationship of the Different Communities of Manipur: A critical Appraisal", Orient Vision, a quarterly journal, Vol.2, Issue 1, October-November-December, 2004, Imphal, p.30.

1. Memo No.1, dated 12 July, 1947 of the Khulmi National Union, submitted to Officials and Naga Tribal Leaders, etc. signed by Teba Kilong, Chairman of the Khulmi National Union.
2. *Zomi Today*, the eight impression, April 1985, Churachandpur.

3. H. Kamkhenthang, "The Paites in the present perspecrtive", *Resistance*, a weekly, Imphal, February 2nd 1977, p.3.
4. *Ibid.*
5. As told by Tangsat Haokip of K. Thenjol village of Singhat on 21.10.2003.
6. *Ibid.*
7. *Ibid.*
8. As told by Lumkhogang, Chairman of Village Authority, D. Phailang Village under Churachandpur Police Station, on 21.10.2003.
9. *Ibid.*
10. *The Kuki-Zomi Conflict: A Synopsis,* issued by the Publicity Wing, Zomi National Volunteers, Manipur Division, Headquarters, Churachandpur, p. 1.
11. *Ibid.*
12. *Critical Analysis of The Kuki Zomi conflicts:* published by The Voice of Churachandpur: Evening Post, not dated, p. 1 and 2.
13. *Ibid*, p.21.
14. *Ibid*, p.22.
15. Group interview with the villagers of Saikul village, Churachandpur, on 18-11-2003.
16. *Critical Analysis of the Zomi-Kuki Conflicts*, op. cit. p. 8.
17. *Ibid.*
18. *Ibid.*, p.9.
19. *Ibid.*, p.18.
20. A compilation by the Information and Publicity Cell of the ZRO.
21. *Ibid.*
22. *The Imphal Free Press,* an English daily, Imphal 22-9-1998.
23. *The Freedom,* an English daily, Imphal 2-10-1998.
24. As told by T. Haokip of Thadou Veng of Singhat, Secy. Village Authority on 9.11.2003.
25. Joint Declaration of July 8th, 1997.
26. *Ibid.*

27. Reaffirmation of Peace Accord, sated July 8, 1997, signed by two signatories each from the side of ZRO/ZRA and the KNF(P).
28. *Ibid.*
29. Cease-fire Agreement, dated August 11th, 1997, signed by Shanada, South Command, KNF(P), on behalf of the KNF(P) and V.K. Joshua, Commander, ZRA, Northern Zone, on behalf of the ZRA.
30. A release issued by Brig. Vipin Haokip, Chief of Army Staff of the Kuki National Army.
31. *The Freedom,* March 9, 1998.
32. *Ibid.*
33. Memorandum of Understanding signed by the Zomi Council and the Kuki Inpi Churachandpur,on 26 March, 1998.
34. *Ibid.*
35. Peace Accord signed on October Ist, 1998, between the Kuki Inpi, Churachandpur and Zomi Council.
36. *Ibid.*
37. *Ibid.*
38. *The Kuki-Zomi Conflict: A Synopsis, op.cit.*
39. Press release issued by the Publicity Wing, Zomi National Volunteers, Manipur Division, Headquarters, Churachandpur, appeared in the *Imphal Free Press,* 10 August, 1997.
40. Pronounced by a special meeting represented by 25 prominent leaders of the Thadou, Paite, Hmar, Mizo, Vaiphei, Gangte and Chongthu tribes, held at the VBA Headquarters on July 6, apepared in The Freedom, July 8, 1997.
41. *The Imphal Free Press*, August 8, 1997.
42. Press release issued by Brig. Vipin Haokip, Chief of Army Staff of the KNA, appeared in the *Imphal Free Press,* July 3, 1997, op.cit.
43. *The Freedom,* November 16, 1997.
44. Thangkhalian Ngaite, Churachandpur, "Divided We Fall", *The Sangai Express,* September 26, 2004.

8

A Comparative Study on Ahom Tai and Meitei Dead Rituals

— L. Suresh Singh

Meitei's are culturally Tai and linguistically Poi. In Meitei we usually encounter many Tai related words. Although there is no comparative genetic studies to sort out what may have been aspects of an original Tai pool among the Meitei when they have formed still a relatively homogenous population along with the Tai community in the Indo-Chinese peninsula. Meitei old manuscripts accounts verify the Typical Tai-ness and more ancient and more indigenous to that of other Tai community. In the case of Meitei and Tai Ahom it become so influenced by the indigenous culture that they eventually lost most of the Tai culture. Historically Meitei account shows about the well-known propensity of the Tainess forming complex socio-political structures and as a people with some assimilative ability and a tendency in the direction of social organization from the time of first historical King Nongda Laipakhangba (33 A.D.). The word Meitei and Meetei is a corrupted word of Mi-Tai (Mei means man in Kabu and Paomei, Tai means tai people) and mei-Tai (mei means man in Kabu-Chin) the name of the early period like Kangmaung' (Maaungkang in Tai) 'Maungba naranyai' Maungba hanjaba. Turel Namshang (Nam means water in Tai) Ching

(Mauntain in Meitei, Highest in Tai) Ching-U (Highly device) Chong (Traditional umbrella in Meitei and Tai Ahom) Khaung or khong (drum in Selloi langmei and in Tai) Magle of moglai name of Meitei of Manipur by the old Assamees (Maunglai' land of lai people) Maungyang Chaoba one of the son of Nongdalai Pakhangba (like Maungkhong Maungyang Kongor khong (kang kong or kang khong wheel in meitei and kong as wheel in Tai Ahom) and Chaobwa in Tai) etc. are all similar to Tai language . The affinity and diversification of Meitei lang uage in my earlier paper and the cultural similarity in the life cycle had been presented in the Manipur University.

In this present paper I am stressing more detail in the Death Ritual of the Tai and Meitei with their affinities. Crimination is widespread among the Meitei and Tai people yet it is unlikely that it constituted one of their Ancient methods of disposal of corpse. In both Ahom Tai and Meitei custom is mainly practised when they had adopted Hindu in Meitei and Buddhist in Tai Ahom faith. But in both the community before the adoption of the new religion burial is the norm. Among the Tai and Chakpa (Kadu- cannan and Thet in Burma) bury the ashes and the remaining bones buried like Pyus.

Tai and Meitei accounts show the existence of four types of disposal of death.

1. Bird burial or bird disposal or Air disposal
2. Water disposal
3. Burial and
4. Crimination

In all the four disposal the two community have close affinities in the crimination of ahom and Meitei are almost similar. In Sakok lamlen Kangbalon the following account are recorded;

"Waram ama khaangnaba haige potloiba haiba di makhal mari shueamadi Nungshit potloi-ne' amadi eeshing potloi-ne namadi leipak potloi-ne amadi meipotloi-ne Meide shithelpharoi-e....

Let me tell one thing to know there are four death disposal one is air disposal one is water disposal one is earth disposal and one is fire disposal fire disposal should not be practice..."

The types of disposal varies according to living status i.e. King, general public, marital status, nature death, and accidental death. Poireiton Khunthokpa manuscript describe about the crimination of Chakpa during his migration from leikha to kanglei. The text shows the fear ness of poireiton with this typed of Fire–disposal. This Leikha from where then Poireiton migrated is at the southern part of Shan state at present and may be the southern part of Nanchao (Southern prince in Chinese" and a part Khakhe in Meitei of Khe country of Tai) .This crimination of the Chakpa is similar to that of That and Pyu death disposals. During the time of king Kangba of Haye Era the method of disposal is said to be Air and bird disposal. The death bodies are disposed in the air and the giant bird Thingpai Ngamba or Kakyel Ngsmba carried away and dropped at the hill range of Heipok hill; Regarding this giant bird the book Biodiversity of South-East Asia mentioned about the discovery of a fossils of giant bird that can carry human being in the 6th century A.D. Bird burial is one of the ancient Tai death disposal. Historical evidence of the Siamese customs and other Tai Death disposal recorded this method of disposal in the name Bird burial. The abandoning corpse to the vultures has been accepted practices the Siam Tai for many centuries. In central Thai at the beginning of the 15th century the death bodies were exposed to the wilds by the Sea side, and subsequently Golden colour birds as large as geese in numbers descend, take the flesh of the copse, devour it completely, and fly away members weep over the bones which remain, then cast them away in the water and return home*

Royal Death rituals

In the case of the dead Meitei kings, unless his successor ascended the throne the death ritual cannot be performed. Naothingkhong Phambal Kaba Text mentioned that when Meitei King, Meidingu Ura Konthouba (568-658) demise the queen Khabarol Nungjengshu call upon his son Naothingkhong from Luwang Makui Ching to succeed his father throne and to performed his father Hongnembe Death ritual. The Death body was kept at the Sumang Khangenpham (courtyard) beating the Royal drums, Cymbal, and Tharaochi mourn for his father. The entire Family member including the noble man dress in while joined the ceremony. In this ceremony the Royal priest informed Kasha Paotakpa or interned to the Anastral land of dead. The new king seat at the Laplen Ka and fruit cock rice are offer to the death. They also offer cloths, eatable things, and sword singing Sana Lam-ook folk song in the rhythms of drum beat and going. They also sing, Hiroi song for the departed soul... Rice, salt, lamp and coins are offered to the celestial God Kasha. The three school of Maibi sanglen the nongmai, Phura and sanglen communicate the decease spirit and offer the articles with ritual songs relating about the departed soul. The death body is kept for five days and offers rice, rice bear, lamb, water and fruit every day. The body is then place in the Kairen Keijao and Koiju dry leave were burned to smoke, a lamp is lighted and performed the rite and rituals. The ritual of Puroi leikoiba, Mathou yangkoiba and Hongnemba are all compulsory ritual procedure for the Kasha Sorarel. The ritual song of Sana lam-ook, Koi-ju lamook, Sanamahi Laihui, Pakhangba Laihui, Ahonglan, Apoklon are also sung but in the general population it differs to some extend.

---

*The Tai of Assam and ancient Tai ritual Vol. 1.

The ceremony of Hongnembba in the death ritual is performed both for the living and the departed soul including the ancestral spirit. In the graveyard from the day of the burial to the next death anniversary the family offer pot of water, a tall bamboo with banners. This type of banner in a tall bamboo in Khamyang Ahom Tai is known as *Taam Khan* or *Wa Caa Ku*. In Meitei small hut is constructed near the burial side and dug out the buried corpse and kept exposed in the hut. Under the Royal division of labour of the clans, performed the secondary burial, first they clean the skull and the remaining part are reburied. The decay part and maggot are removed next by next and washed several time and fixed together are the part and dry the skull in the sun. Hongnemba ritual ceremony is again performed decorating the skull with gold or silver according to the status of the Family. For the kings gold mask is compulsory. The decorated skull is reburied as secondary burial. In many excavations by the archeology department, the secondary burial. In many excavations by the archeology department, the secondary burial encounter with gold mask in the skull is a typical Meitei secondary burial but not that of Pyus or Burmese. The Pyus burial is urn ash secondary burial. Golden artifacts ornated with the motifs of Buddhist cult once offer as gift to the spirit are always misinterpreted by many scholars as an extension of Pyus and Mao-Shan secondary burrials. But comparative studies of the Mainland South East Asian cultures reveal that these are the artifacts collected during the war with Burmese or Shans in early period. Manipuries are hardly influence by Buddhist religion. The Puroi Mashil manuscript clearly mentioned about the secondary burial with decoration from the early period.

There exists a nineteenth century description about the Shan burial custom the Chaos (Kings) and official of rank are generally buried. The body is embalmed and kept above the ground for several months, during which period the friends and relatives are entertained. The face of the dead chao is invariably covered with a mask of gold and silver. In Ahom Rajadhon in his the folk religion of Ban Nai mentioned that rich person covered their face with golden mask and for ordinary people used a mask made of beeswax.

Chiefs of Shan, Yuan, Thai and Lao wear a golden mask, or have their face gilded with gold leaf.

The Construction of Mortuary House

Construction of mortuary house are fairly widespread among the Tai. The used of canopy on the top of the coffin is also found on the Tai graves. In ahom Tai for rich people or noble man construct tombs as spectacular Tai mortuary houses. Construction of earthen mount and canopy above the coffin or grave is also found in Meiteis like the Tais.

The Coffin

In general the Tai place dead in the oblong wooden coffin. The oldest descriptions of coffins are refer to a hollowed out trunk like the ancient Meitei practices. Rajadhon's idea that the coffin originally may have had the shape of a drug-out canoe is similar to the used of canoe by the Moirang people which was found accidentally at loktak lake. The custom of canoe and hollowed out tree truck as coffin in is quite widespread in South-East Asia.

In addition; the Tai and Meitei there is a widespread custom of ritual wailing after at the moment when the wake end and the coffin leaves the house. The two communities share this formal expression of grief with many other peoples.

Leaving the House

Two of the most widespread customs amongst the Tai are the preparation of a special spirit ladder with an even number of rum to be used only for the removal of the coffin and lowering of the coffin through especially prepared hole in the wall. The customs of destroying one or more water pot or containers at the moment of living the house is quite widespread among the Tai. The ritual destruction of other goods which are considered given to the decease at various stages of the funeral it also contains earthen pots presented to the spirit as a farewell gesture. This type of custom and believed is found in the Meitei custom. In Meitei the dead body is removed body is removed through the khagenpham and a cotton thread is stretched thread is stretched from the naktha to the corner of the courtyard where the body is to be kept. This thread is to transport the soul of the decease and for the next transportation the thread is again stretch upto the graveyard. If the graveyard is at a great distance the threat is stretch upto the graveyard. If the graveyard is at a great distance the threat is stretch when the coffin is about to reach the burial side. This type of stretching the threat is still practiced among the Ahom and other Tais. At the time of transpiration of the copse the doors and windows except the back doors are close. The underlying philosophy is that the house is taken as human body in which the backdoor is the opening of the female organ' opening of this door invite the spirit for rebirth.

Procession

The Tai funeral processions demonstrate considerable with regard to the other of people. In some case the male lead the procession and in case of other the women lead the procession. But in Meitei the group of ritual singer with the drums cymbal lead the procession and them the man with fire in a earthen pot and the coffin next the Male family members and the female and other man and women follows the procession.

Yet there are some regularity which may have bearing on ancient Tai ritual. The customs of connecting the coffin or bier with thread and letting some ritually superior persons hold this thread is remarkable widespread like the intri Meites*

---

*Tai Death rituals in wider context, The Tai of Assam and ancient Tai ritual. Vol-1, p. 155. by B. J. Tarwiel.

Funeral masts

Quite widespread among the Tai is the use of some kind of funeral masts. Among the Ahom Tai The Sham White and black Tai and the Nung a long bamboo poles holding banners is also one of the important ritual item. Pageno. 159' The Tai of Assam and Ancient Tai ritual. The use of a long bamboo pole with banner is mentioned in the Naothingkhong Phampal Kaba. Basically the Khwan or life vital elements joint to the other would through this bamboo poles.

Purification

According to B. J. Terwiel there are a series of interesting purification rituals performed after the funeral. This include a ritual cleaning and washing of the house. Those persons who participate the funeral rituals bath and wash the cloths, and go near the fire and thorny branches. The purification rituals in Meitei are almost the same with the Tais with slight variation. Among the Ahom Tai a new Kitchen is laid which is similar to the Meitei's removal of the ash and charcoals and cleaning the fire place, use of new pots breaking of the earthen pots.

Abstain from cocking

Among the Tai including the Assamese Tai the members of the deceased's clan must mourn and abstain cocking for there days until the ritual purification has taken place. During this ceremony offering are made to the ancestors and some food is place on the burial mound under a small shed constructed specially for that purpose. In Meitei, the abstain from cocking is shorter than the other Tais, they abstain the whole day or until the crimination is completed.

Putting of coins

The give of coin is virtually ubiquitous amongst the Tai and Meitei and appears to be part of the Ancient rituals. In most accounts the coin is placed in the deceased's mouth' but in a few cases it is tucked under the neck or simply put at the hand in the coffin.

The idea that money will be needed when the deceased travels to the other would and when he has to cross a river in the process is fairly widespread. The custom of placing a coin in the mouth among the Tais and Meitei may not be regarded as uniquely Tai. It has been reported for Tai-related groups such as the li, the Laqua, and many Kuki-chin people including Lushai.

In Ahom and Tai in general and Meitei death ritual similarities

1. Upon death the death body received a though washing with boiled water.
2. There are at least three types of burial system before the influence other religion. This includes air and bird disposal; water disposal, and earth disposal.
3. A coin was given to the decease likely place in the mouth as a fair to the way of the land of dead.
4. The corpse was fully dress and it is likely that some covering was used. The coffin may be a hollowed out tree trunk or a canoe.
5. The offering of animal lamp rice canopy bamboo poles with banner.
6. The used of golden mask on the face in the royal death rituals.
7. At the end of the funeral the living underwent a ritual purification.
8. The ritual experts or specialist was needed to guide the spirit safely to the world of death.

REFERENCE

Kangbarol

Meitei Hongnemba Amasung Ukrong Hongba, by Chiteshwar Shrama.

Naothingkhong Phambal Kaba, M.S.

Puroi Mashil, M.S.

Shinkumlon, M.S.

Shakok Lamlen Ahanba.

Tai Culture: International Review on Tai Cultural Student Bangkok, Vol. iii. No.1.

Tai-Ahom: Religion and Customs, by, Dr. Padmeswar Coroi.

The Tai of Assam and Ancient Tai Rutual, Vol 1 by B. J. Terwiel.

9

Social Integration in Early Manipur: Some Aspects

— Amal Sanasam

At the very outset I would like to say that I am sociologist I have traveled to many places in and outside Manipuri. I am fascinated by the many facets of Manipur society. My visit to Andro, Ningel, Waithou, Moirang, Tamenglong, Chandel, Senapati, Kakching and several villages have compelled me to look into some of the problems which our society is facing today. Recently we have witnessed a social movement of an unprecedented kind. The Manipuri society acted in unison for the removal of AFSPA. It presented a type of integrated social movement led by the different social and civil groups, student and teenagers alike. I was overwhelmed by the show of various social forces, which had come together during this period. Sometime back there was tension between the hill and the plain on account of a would be political decision of integrating the Naga dominated territories of Manipur with Nagaland. This was considered to be an inflammatory decision. The people of Manipur rose against this singularly and since then the problem of social integration between the hill and the valley, between different communities, have come to the fore. It is in the light of these developments that I thought to present this paper on- Social integration that existed in the past and its ramifications in the present.

My paper deals with the factors responsible for social integration in ancient Manipur.

In a widely acclaimed paper of Shri Bhuvan Singh 'Whither Manipur?' one can get a glimpse of a common man's desire to keep the Manipuri society integrated. Not longtime ago the hill people called the 'Chingmee' and the valley people called 'Tammee' had been interacting freely and with social responsibility in the past when the Manipuri society was fragmented. There were several clans and people who were living across the state. Any person could stay in any pana provided his loyalty to the ruling Chiefs. But mainly the seven clans – the Ningthouja, Khuman, Angom, Khaba-Nganba, Chenglei and Moirang were more responsible for bringing about integration. Some of the ethno historical factors have been analysed in detail in my thesis where in I have highlighted that the chief of various ethnic communities worked together to bring about a socio political change. In the Pre-Pakhangba period we hear of Khaba-Nganba who controlled Kangla. The principality of Moirang was well established, their literature –'Moirang Ningthourol Lambuba has suggested that their society had acquired dynamism and was ready to take up socio-political challenges in their stride. Pakhangba was also compelled, or it may have been out of his volition that he took shelter with the Moirangs. It was in pursuit of power that he had taken shelter. But soon after a dynamic history unfolded. It was a period of turmoil. Ethnic communities were asserting for power and territory. Pakhangba emerged as the Sovereign. He controlled through aggressive policies and appeasement. Through matrimonial alliances he tried to consolidate and strengthened social ties between various communities – the Angoms, Mangang, Luwang and the Moirangs. Pakhangba was invited by Puleiromba, the Angom Chief, Luwang Langmaiba of Luwang, Ninthem Apanba of the Mangang and many leaders of Chakpa tribe to come to the Kangla the ancient capital of the Meitei kingdom.[1]

Many tribal villages Leshi,Thangwai, Mucheng,Keihon, Naokal, Haomu, Tangkhul whose villagers extended help and followed him upto Kangla at the time of coronation ceremony[2]. Pakhangba became the recognized head of the Meitei confederacy; only the Khumans and Moirangs remained out of the confederacy. But in the social affairs, the Khuman and Moirangs had also come under the fold of the Meiteis, though political autonomy was retained by them for several centuries and they yielded only after lot of initial resistance.

The greatest achievement of Nongda Lairen Pakhangba was the social consolidation of the different ethnic groups and tribes under the seven clans- the Luwangs, Angoms, Mangang (later on Ningthouja), the Khabas, Nganbas, Sarang Leishangthem (Chenglei), the Khumans and the Moirang. They came under the Meitei social confederacy. The social integration of these tribes provided the strongest political support to Pakhangba's Kingdom. Thus an integrated nucleus was formed on which lay the responsibility of bringing about a socially integrated transformation in the face of antagonism shown by other communities in the valley. Integration and disintegration of various ethnic communities went on simultaneously.

Conservatism too was a force, which needed to be overcome. The Ningthouja could see this dimension and so worked towards the realisation of a unified Manipurs State. They encountered many hurdles in the process but succeed by the end of the 15th century to forge a kind of political stability for the formation of a state.

Pakhangba married Poireiton's sister Leisna in order to allowed other communities to have a say in the sharing of power and also integrating several other communities. At that time the society in this part of the North East was simplistic, not very complex. There were no barriers in form of marriage relationships between the hill and the valley people. Many of the Ningthous of the valley had wives from the hills and vice versa.

Interestingly the relationship of Naothingkhong and Shelloi Langmai girl named Pitanga is also another formidable one. In order to escape the wrath of his father (Urakonthouba) who was a strict disciplinarian and very conscious of education, Naothingkhong ran away from the Kangla and went to live along the Shelloi Langmais in Nongmaiching hills to the East of the kingdom. The two got married, however, after Naothinkhong became the king, he did not make Pitanga his chief queen. So Pitanga died of shock but she was later worshipped as Yumjao Leima by the order of king Naothingkhong.[3] Wagbren, one of the nine deities who protect the south direction married an Anal lady. At present there is a shrine of Wangbren in Chandel. It is because of their belief that the Anal offer cloth at the temple of Wangbren at the time of merrymaking of the said Meitei diety. So they consider it their duty even today to gift a cloth at this function in the name of the Anal girl.[4]

Rules that any Meitei king who had marriage relationship with hill tribes were debarred from the Kangla enclosures emerged much later. The relation of Meitei king Paikhomba and Ingalei, which is portrayed in folk tales and song, is a notable one. Ingalei is a daughter of a hill chief. This story may be a fabled one but is very close to reality. It is often sung in Khongjom Parva and Khunung Isei Similarly several individual heroes of the Meiteis married into the hill clans. So gradually a symbiotic relationship developed which have left behind indelible mark upon our society. These marriage factors directly or indirectly, played a definite role in the process of state formation and integration of the Manipuri society. It was a welcome phenomena.

. Gangumei Kabui, R.K Jhalajit, W.Ibohal Singh, N. Khelchandra and many others, Bhuvan Singh included have given ample evidence to this fact that the Meiteis had very strong relationship with the hill people, and *vice versa.*

Gangmumei Kabui in his book Jadonang a Mystic Naga Rebel[5] emphasis that the Meitei connection with the Zeliangrong is quite ancient. Zeliangrong is comprised of Zemei, Liangnei and Rongmei. The Meitei chronicle and historical texts of Manipur refer to the relation between the two peoples. The Tamenglong hills, its stiff mountains and dense forests provided shelter to the fleeing Meitei princes during their repeated rebellions against the state authorities and during invasions from Burma. The Zeliangrong relations with the kings of Moirang in Southern Manipur valley are found in the famous Khamba-Thoibi epic of Moirang and in their folklore. There were repeated military conflicts between the Meitei rulers and the Zeliangrong village of Koubru Leimaton range and the Ijei and Leimatak Basins. The Zeliangrong village chiefs helped king Garib Niwaz of Manipur during his Burma-wars in the first half of the 18th century. His grandson king Bhagyachandra also took shelter in Zeliangrong country during his liberation struggle against the Burmese.

R.K Jhalajit stated that in medieval times, the people of Manipur had to defend their frontiers from Burmese invasions. In medieval times, not only Burma but also neighbouring Cachar and nearby Tripura occasionally invaded Manipur. The Manipuris had to repel these invasions also. If Manipur had remained divided into seven main principalities and innumerable hill villages, it would have been impossible to defend Manipur from the invading people. Integration of Manipur was a must. He further states in the sixth century, in the reign of Sameirang the Ningthouja principality embarked on the process of conquering and integrating the other principalities and the hill areas. In the seventh century, only Luwang, Khuman and Moirang principalities remained independent of the Ningthouja Kingdom. In the hills, nearly all the hill areas between Cachar and the Manipur valley became a part of the Ningthouja

Kingdom[6] as they began paying some kind of tribute regularly.

Let us see some of the traditional beliefs. The Chief (Khullakpa) of Hundung, a place in Ukhrul had two sons. One day the younger brother left home to search his lost pig. On a particular place called Oknaopokpi (at present called Yangangpokpi) he found his pig giving birth to many piglets, and as a reason of it he couldn't come back home .The elder brother got disappointed and decided to search his brother. The two brothers met at the place. The younger brother requested that he would rule in the valley. He promised that in the month of October. (Mera) a bamboo will be erected with a lamp on top of it. That would show that he was still alive. After one year had passed the elder brother brought a present 'Panao Senao' to be given to his brother. Even today this gift is given which has become an indispensable item in marriage ceremony of Meitei community. The two brothers met each other happily and a celebration was held, which is known as Mera Haochongba. This festival symbolizes peace happiness and togetherness. Even today it is celebrated in the spirit of love and affection for each other.

Some of the Puyas of Manipur tell us that the clan of the Angom is believed to have migrated from the northeast from the Kangkhui caves near Ukhrul. It is believed that they might have lived for some time in the caves of Kangkhui, which provided temporary shelter to the migrating people. Quite similar is the legend of two brothers Angoupa and Chingsomba who came out of the Khangkhui caves. Chingsomba the elder brother went to the land of the Thangal tribe in the north and his younger brother, Angouba, came to Kangla where the throne was vacant[8].

Another origin theory makes us believed that people of hill and valley originated from Khebu, the plateau of Makan, on the northern side of Manipur . A big tree was grown on this plateau. From that tree three brothers departed in three direction - North, East, South. They promised not to see each other again. The eldest brother who went to the East formed Tangkhuls, the second brother who had gone to the Northern side formed Ngamei(Angami) and the third one who had gone to South formed the Meitei. This particular place Khebu was known by the Meitei as 'Khebu Ching'.[9] Angami called it as 'Japhu'. The people of Mao and Maram called it as 'Khephu'. Thus a common origin of these groups can be established in this legend.

On account of an emotional feeling the elder brother broke his promise and looked to his younger brother. At the same time the later also looked back. Then the younger called to his elder brother 'Iyamba'. The elder brother responded with 'Hao'. Since then, it is believed that the hill people were called as 'Hao'.

The youngest brother according to Kangbarol puya is supposed to be the king Kangba.[10] It is alleged that he came down from the hills and settled at Kangpokpi for some time. He waited till the water receded from the valley. Later, he shifted to Kanglatongbi. As the water receded further he came down to Kangjabi where a big feast was held and two stones were erected. These could be the demarcation of their boundary. Legend says that later he shifted his capital to Kangamong. Perhaps environmental factors made him migrate to more safer and congenial places. However, the fact that he was migrating from one place to another also testifies that he was establishing groups of people in these areas. Some integration of the territory was also taking place cannot be ruled out.

Likewise the common traditional story of Konthoujam Lairema is very similar to Dailelieu of Gonthangmei clan of Kabui tribe. Such traditional beliefs and folklore show and make us believe that the hill and the plain people had intimate relationships. They were supplementary and complementary to each other. They interacted together to meet their needs.

These hearsay and folklore are common to both the communities. Infact when we look deeper into the cultural aspect of Manipur we find integration of many of their traits.

For examples in every home of Kabui, Koireng, Kom etc. one will find Sanamahi and Leimaran(house hold deities) as can be found in any Meitei household. Bhuvan Singh in his article[11] states that the Kabuis and Kirengs observe Ningol Chakaoba (feasting of sisters) just like the Meiteis. Hamei an issential item use in marriage ceremony of Meitei is also used in tribal community. Leirum a distinctive Tangkhul blanket is a must in the dowry of a Meitei girl. M.Kirti Singh's seminar paper[12] on Paphal cult statesthat the Meiteis and the hill tribes lived in intimate contact with pythons, dragons and snakes, and for them they are not dumb creatures of primitive faith but divine beings more or less ancestors of the clans.

With respect to the formation of clans, yeks and salais the old tribes of Manipur like the Maring, the Tangkhul, the Kabui, the Chothe, the Kom, Moyon, Koireng appear to have developed seven clans or sageis on a similar pattern like that of the Meiteis.[13]

McCulloch also emphasis to a close social and cultural relationship between Meitei clans or tribes with the adjacent hill tribes-like the Tangkhul relation with the Angoms and Khaba-Nganbas, the Khuman connection with the Marings and the Anals, Luwang connections with the Kabuis and other tribe like Kom,Chirus and Koirang.[14]

Without differentiating between the Naga and the Kuki clans (which were made perhaps sometime during the colonial period), we would like to assert, that the clan formation and the sub clans growing into clans is the process of development as social dynamics inherent in the formation of a clan itself which followed exogamous forms of marriage. Sub clans got elevated to clan level when similar sub clans got merged through these matrimonial alliances in order to become a

Tribes	1	2	3	4	5	6	7
Tangkhuls	Khudang	Khopudang	Sithudang	Choudang	Kingdang	Duidang	Sadang
Maring	Sampen	Raj	Dalla	Dingthoi	Chingdur	Thanganga	Thoitak
Kabui	Kammei	Gangmei	Longmei	Maringmei	Golmei	Phaomei	Palmei
Moyon-	Nungru	Bungouhei	Sirbum	Ruin	Chiru	Segong	Songsher
Monshang	Langrom	Cham	Turip	Nangaran	Nungchin	Hungam	Khartur
Anal	Nurchal	Pasen	Masem	Chanting	Runval	Hrangung	Yasha
Koireng	Miple	Leison	Sonthu	Yeite	Tumtin	Walbe	Tonti

(as given in W. Iboha *The History of Manipur*)

social and a political power. In the early period we have seen small groups form into clans and sub clans when they were seen integrating or disintegrating on accounts of their inherent contradictions.

Here, I would like to emphasize that after the Pakhangba raid on the Kangla, the Khaba-Nganbas had been forced to hand over their fort - the Kangla. Many of them were forced to runaway. They took shelter in different direction but especially in the hills. They gradually, and over the centuries forged themselves as different/separate clans who had their settlements in the hills. A close look into the writings of Shri B. Kulachandra Sharma would make it clear that the clans and sub clans, which developed, had common origin. He discusses the numerous tribes of the plain people as is recorded by the Meitei Puyas with their ethnic groups and their composition.

For example the ***Chenglei*** comprise of the Kang, Chenglei, Urok,Ushai, Songpu, Leishang, Sarang, Potsangba, Lokoton, Haorok and Konthou. The ***Khaba-Nganba*** comprised of Khaba, Nganba, Khumukcha, Nongchengs and Longkhumus. Likewise the breaks up of other clans are also recorded.[15]

In the coronation ceremony of the kings of Manipur we find several traits, which are common to both the hill and the plain people. Social integration was taking place through festivals like Laiharaoba, Haochongba, etc. It brought the different communities together on several occasions, annually and periodically. It was also because of their interaction during the harvest of agriculture crops that the people came together interacted vigorously and picked up words, which are common to their societies. This was beginning of having a common language, which could be understood by the majority of the people. Meiteilon is not only understood by the hill people but is also spoken by them. Here, one thing is important to note and that is when individual adopted incestuous relationship or committed grievous crime they were ostracized to the hills. They also became agents of social change. They carried their culture along with them to far off places in the interior of Manipur hills. They established settlement, which became centers of civilized groups from where again culture spread. Directly or indirectly such policies of state, which discriminated against individuals contributed towards social integration in remote places.

The best example of social and political integration can be seen in the manuscript Kangla Houba, where we find that for the construction of palace hall-pillars were brought by the chiefs of different ethnic communities from their respective localities. Special type of wood was preferred. It was stated that the main pillar of Kangla should be made from the wood of particular tree, **Haiyukhok** found in the Koubru hills. The pillar opposite to the main pillar was to be made from the wood of **Chingthang Upan** available in the **Chingkhei** hills. The wood for the pillar next to the main pillar again was brought from **Wangbren** hill. The wood for its opposite pillar made from **Tumitla** tree was brought from **Pishum** hills. The next pillar was made from the wood of **Taimeran** brought from **Langing Ching** and the next pillar, opposite to this pillar, was brought from **Chingthang**. **Ukhoten,** which was the name of a pillar, was brought from **Heibok** hill. **Kangla,** which was a name of a beam, was brought from **Khebu ching**. **Ura-Umdang** (Kanchi), which was a typical bamboo, was collected from **Thanga Karam**.

Charot of thatch roofing was obtained from **Langmaijing** hills. **Paya** (bamboo ribon) was obtained from **Wabagai**. **Sanayumbi**, another pillar, was brought from **Thanging** hills. **Khangen**, another beam, was collected from **Langol hills**. The four pillars for the four directions was to be brought from the four panas- **Ahallup, Naharup, Khabam** and **Laipham**. Later these panas were renamed as **Leikais- Khwai, Yaiskul, Khurai** and **Wangkhei**

respectively. The chiefs of these leikais were made responsible for the collection of different kinds of wood as mentioned above, whenever the need arose.[16]

It appears that this arrangement of constructing Kangla from woods brought from different places was an attempt to integrate and consolidate the people living in the valley along with the people of the hills. This settlement pattern was singular and effectively maintained since Kangla was the capital of the many ethnic communities so each of them had to share their wealth with a sense of responsibility. Kangla developed as a common heritage.

At the end, when one decide to make one's home in another country, one must do his best to conform to rules of the society in which one live and integrate with the mainstream. Likewise, in the later period of Garibniwaj, the hill tribals and the Mayang became loyal to the king. The kings' sons and grandsons got married to the descendants of the hill tribes and Mayangs. Gradually, the profession of serving the Gods of the Kings also allowed to the hill tribes and Mayangs. Many posts were also given according to their skill. Many hill people came to the plain and got absorbed in different clans and sub clans of the Meiteis. Kerio a manuscript gives us some instances. The Soibam sub clan settled in Phoijing Chingmei belonged to Maring tribe. The Moirangthem settled in Langsombi belonged to Kabui Haochong tribe. The Kollom, Akangjam settled at Takyel and the Karam, Arambam settled at Sagolband were from Achep tribe. The Haobism settled at Yurenjam and Thounoujam belonged to haokei tribe. The Waribam, Konjengbam, Thoudam of Khurai belonged to Nongchup tribe. The Akoijam of Thoubal were from the Maring tribe. The Konsam of Khurai were from Kabow. The Yanglem of Samurou belonged to the Marring tribe. The Leitanthem and Mangsatabam of Thoubal belonged to Tangkhul. The Thongam, Chanam, Khogjam of Thiyam belonged to Chingshang tribe.[17] Thus we see that there was an attempt to integrate people belonging to different tribes who came into the fold of the process of integration in the valley which was at full swing during the 15th and 16th century AD.

Conclusion

I would like to maintain that it is very much imperative for the different component of our society to get integrated once again as I find that instead of remaining integrated, our society is revealing fragmentation, and assertion of all communities feelings in term of social identity. People are adopting titles. which speak of their yek or salai.

My hope is that we will remain as a plate of salad with different components having different identity but integrated. What I mean is that we should have unity in diversity and as it existed in the past we should forge ahead a fraternity of equality and freedom within a composite society. Our aim should be to retain all the people residing in the hills or the valley and the territory, which they occupy because traditionally it has belonged to all of us, together.

NOTES

1. Kh. Yaima, *Pakhanba Phambal* pp.26-27.
2. Gangmumei Kabui, *History of Manipur* Vol.1 p.84.
3. N. Khelchandra Singh, *Naothingkhong Phambal Kaba*, pp.5-6.
4. Mutua Bahadur, *Tribal hand Woven Fabrics of Manipur*, p.120.
5. p. 8.
6. R.K. Jhalajit Singh, *History of Medieval India*, Seminar paper.
7. Atompapu Sharma, *Pakhangba*, pp.243-245.
8. Gangmumei Kabui, *History of Manipur* Vol.1, p.155.
9. Kh. Yaima, *Anoirol.*
10. L. Nitai, *Kangbarol.*
11. H. Bhuvan Singh, *Whither Manipur?*, Seminar paper.

12. M. Kirti Singh, *Paphal Cult - A peeps into its cultural values*, Seminar Paper.
13. W. Ibohal Singh, *The History of Manipur*, p.609.
14. M McCulloch, *Account of the valley of the Manipur*, p.4.
15. B. Kulachandra Sharma, *Ancient Etnic Groups of Manipur Valley up to 1500AD*, Seminar paper.
16. N. Khelchandra Singh, *Ariba Manipuri Shahityagi Itihas*. p.69.
17. Sagei Salairol, *Manipuri Sate Kala Academy*, pp.166-176.

Index

F

G

H

I

J

K

L